SPARK OF HOPE

AN AUTOBIOGRAPHY

LUBA WROBEL GOLDBERG

ISBN 9789493322776 (ebook)

ISBN 9789493322783 (paperback)

ISBN 9789493322790 (hardcover)

Publisher: Amsterdam Publishers, The Netherlands

info@amsterdampublishers.com

A Spark of Hope is part of the series Holocaust Survivor Memoirs World War II

Revised and expanded edition of *A Spark of Hope. An Autobiography* (2007)

Edited by Fiona Kelmann (granddaughter of Luba Goldberg) 2024

Copyright © Brian Goldberg, 2024

Cover image: Luba and Chaim Goldberg, Melbourne, circa 1949

All Rights Reserved. No part of this publication may be reproduced or transmitted in any form or by any means, electronic or mechanical, including photocopy, recording or any other information storage and retrieval system, without prior permission in writing from the publisher.

CONTENTS

Acknowledgments   v
Preface   vii

PART I

My Hometown - Ciechanowiec, Poland	3
Childhood Memories	10
My Family	13
School Years	18
A Jewish Mother's Worry	25
The Holy Man	29
My Years in Bialystok	32
The Nazi Invasion of Poland	37
Under Russian Occupation	39
The Germans return	45
Life in Sokoly Ghetto	51
News of Nazi Atrocities nearby	60
We flee to the Forest	62
Wanderings	76
Narrow Escapes	87
With the Partisans	103
Spark of Hope	111
The Germans attack	116
Counteractions	120
With the Jews from Bransk	125
Missions with the Russian Partisans	136
More Sparks of Hope	145
Bialystok	162
The Fate of My Family	166
In Search of a Future	177

PART II

Our Arrival in Australia	189
Life in Fitzroy, Melbourne	195
Mitchell Street, Brunswick, Melbourne	202
The Hardships of Starting a Tiny Factory	206

Our Corner Shop	210
Mozart Street, St Kilda	215
My Children grow up	218
Reunion in Israel 1971	227
Epilogue	233
My message	237
Photos	239
Amsterdam Publishers Holocaust Library	253

ACKNOWLEDGMENTS

I must include a thank you to my grandson, Brian Goldberg, for assisting me to write and publish my memoirs.

I would also like to thank my granddaughter, Fiona Kelmann, for her encouragement, patience, and assistance in guiding me whilst writing this book.

I would like to dedicate this book to the six million innocent Jewish victims of the Holocaust – babies, children, women, men and the elderly – whose stories can never be told.

PREFACE

Spark of Hope is an autobiography that records the story of my early childhood and life in pre-World War II Poland, how I survived the Holocaust, the fate of my family, and my postwar life. It is also a brief account of my trials and tribulations starting life anew in my adopted country of Australia, and the joys I experienced in raising a family of my own – my little victory over those who dared to think they could erase the memory of my people and extinguish our Jewish heritage.

I hope and believe that knowledge of my painful experiences will contribute to, and benefit the world. Old and young readers alike will understand how racial hatred can contribute to so much unhappiness and suffering for millions of innocent people.

I pray that in the future, every one of us will work towards peace and happiness for all people of all faiths, color and creed, everywhere.

Luba Wrobel Goldberg

Melbourne, Australia

PART I

MY HOMETOWN - CIECHANOWIEC, POLAND

My name is Luba. It means "dear" or "loved" in Yiddish, the main language that Jews in Eastern Europe spoke before World War II. I was born in 1923 to a Jewish family in Ciechanowiec, a sizeable town, near Bialystok in Poland. All Jews in Ciechanowiec spoke Yiddish and many also spoke Polish, Russian, and other languages. Ciechanowiec was a very ancient town, believed to have been founded in the tenth century. Jews had lived in Ciechanowiec for many centuries, and it is thought to be one of the oldest Jewish communities in Poland. There were a couple of thousand Jews who lived in Ciechanowiec before the war; they constituted about 60 percent of the town's total population.

Ciechanowiec itself was divided into two by the Nurzec River, which flows into the Bug River. The side where we lived was called the "old" or "Polish" town. There was a big bridge over the Nurzec River, and on the other side of it was the "new" or "Russian" town. During World War I, the Nurzec River marked the border between Poland and Russia.

My hometown was surrounded by forests, which stretched all the way to other towns, such as Wysokie and Czyzewo to the north, and Bransk and Bielsk to the east. Ciechanowiec was located between several rivers and was very beautiful; a picturesque, charming rural town. It was a popular place for people from other cities to come for picnics, hiking, swimming, and other outdoor activities. Some came for their summer vacation.

My mother's family had lived in Ciechanowiec and the surrounding areas for many generations. I believe my father's family, the Wrobels, had lived there for several hundred years and I think they had always practiced the trade of wheelwrights, which continued to be a useful trade in Ciechanowiec even when I was growing up as there were no cars. There were trains to travel between the bigger cities and there was a train to the nearby big cities of Bialystok and Warsaw, but for day-to-day travel, the townsfolk used horses and wagons. So, for example, when the farmers came into the town, they came by horse and cart; when a merchant wished to sell his goods in another town, he traveled by horse and wagon. This was the case even on the eve of the war.

There was a distinct Jewish settlement in Ciechanowiec known as a *shtetl*. In Eastern Europe, *shtetlach* (plural in Yiddish) existed in many rural areas. Overall, even though some people in my hometown were wealthy, most were not, and in fact, many were extremely poor. And yet, everyone, regardless of whether they were wealthy or not, was very conscious of giving to charity and helping fellow Jews in the shtetl who were less fortunate. There was even an orphanage where the children were educated and taught trades, allowing them to be independent members of society when they grew up. There was also an old age home that was funded by the community leadership of the shtetl. People tried to help the less fortunate by cooking for them and inviting them to a Sabbath meal.

Most Jews in my shtetl attended synagogue on the Jewish holidays and observed the sabbath and *kashrut* [Jewish dietary laws]. There was a main synagogue as well as smaller ones known as *shtiebels*. Most of the Jews in my shtetl were not overly religious as may have been the case in other shtetlach, but they clung to the traditions and some did not even speak Polish well, speaking only Yiddish.

Most of the men were engaged in work, unlike other Jewish communities elsewhere in Poland where they only studied *Torah* and *did* not work. Additionally, all the women worked too, out of necessity.

When I was born, the shtetl was going through a transformative phase as a response to modernization and industrialization, but also to existing antisemitism. The new generation was becoming less observant and less conservative than the older generation. Many young people became influenced by popular political movements of the day and wanted to completely secularize. Some, mainly younger members of the shtetl, had left to seek out opportunities in bigger cities in Poland and abroad.

Zionism was popular in our shtetl and in 1930s, as a response to rising antisemitism in Poland, most young people joined Zionist youth movements. My father's brother, Abram-Moshele Wrobel, married a girl from Bialystok in the early 1930s. They used the dowry money to go and live in Mandatory Palestine. When I was a young girl, I belonged to a Zionist youth movement where we sang songs in Hebrew and dreamed of a Jewish state in the land of Israel. There were several Zionist youth movements that operated in Ciechanowiec and most of them believed in creating a socialist Jewish state in Mandatory Palestine. I also helped to collect money for the Jewish National Fund which assisted Jews settling there. Ciechanowiec was known for its generous contribution to the Jewish National Fund, even though it had such a small and mainly poor Jewish population.

Despite modernization slowly creeping in, the shtetl was a time capsule in many ways. People lived there pretty much as they had for hundreds of years. Not too much had changed; physical conditions were quite primitive but that was the norm for rural areas in Poland; there was no electricity, no paved roads, houses were generally wooden and small. Most houses doubled as workplaces where people sold, made, or fixed goods and were built close to the street so that customers could enter easily.

There was no plumbing in the houses; most of our water came from the different rivers nearby. We used different rivers for different purposes: there was one spot on the bank of one of the rivers where the townsfolk used to wash the dishes, pots and pans; as children, we were sent to the river to scrub the dishes with sand and grass and when the dishes were clean, we rinsed them in the river; in a different, deeper part of the river, the women rinsed their washed laundry; another river was used only for bathing and swimming.

We had to bring buckets of water from the well, about 300 meters away from our house. The water was drawn from the well in a wooden pail attached to the well and then poured into our buckets. Some of the water would often spill in the process. The ground around the well was usually wet.

Winters were very cold in Ciechanowiec. It was, on average, about 40 degrees Celsius below zero. We wore felt boots with rubber overshoes called galoshes as it was slippery and dangerous to walk in that weather.

In winter 1932, my paternal grandmother, Alte Reva Wrobel went to the well to fetch water. The well was on a hill and the water had spilled gathered in puddles and froze into ice around it, making the ground very slippery. My grandmother slipped on the ice at the well and in falling, broke her leg. The doctor in our town couldn't set the leg so he sent grandmother to a hospital in Warsaw.

I remember my Auntie Basia telling us how she saw my grandmother lying in a hospital bed, with her broken leg attached to the ceiling. The leg healed, but it was left shorter than the other one. When my grandmother walked, it was very funny to see. I knew I shouldn't have laughed, but I couldn't help it. Whenever I saw her walk from behind, I laughed. She would put her good leg forward and then make a half-twisting motion with the shorter leg, like a dancing step. Eventually, we became accustomed to seeing her walk that way. After her accident, she always wore long skirts.

We used large, heavy, cast-iron pots that fitted half inside the fire in the stove and half on top for cooking. We needed to light the fire with wood as there was no gas or electricity in our homes. Because my father was a wheelwright, we were lucky enough to have dry wood for fuel and we cooked with the chips and splinters from his workshop. Women from our side of town would come to our workshop to gather free chips and splinters in their aprons to use in lighting their fires, because their firewood was not always dry.

On the Sabbath we used the bakery's oven as a communal oven for the Sabbath cholent, a traditional meat and bean stew. My grandmother was in charge of the cholent. I used to walk with her to the bakery and we gave our heavy pot to the baker to put in the oven overnight to cook slowly. The next day we would come to collect the hot cholent for the Sabbath lunch. All the pots looked similar to me, but my grandmother never got confused and always knew which one was ours.

Eighty percent of the population of Ciechanowiec were skilled tradesmen. Most of them worked for themselves, out of their own homes. They were tailors, shoemakers, wheelwrights, blacksmiths, string-makers, furriers, glaziers, carpenters, harness-makers, saddlers, turners, hat-makers. Others would hire workers for a harvest season and sell the harvested fruit.

Some people had small vegetable gardens and sold their produce in market stalls. There were also a few bakeries, groceries, haberdashery shops, fabric shops, and more. Twice a week there were market days when farmers from the surrounding villages would come to sell their produce and buy other goods. The women in town would buy chickens, eggs, and butter from the farmers and sell these at a small profit to larger traders, who then packed them in cases and sent them by train to Warsaw, the largest city in Poland.

There were very large market fairs in our town twice a year. These fairs were the main source of income for nearly everyone; farmers and traders used to come from all over Poland to buy or sell horses and cattle. Everybody worked hard during the months between fairs, and when the time came, they displayed their wares on the streets in front of their workshops. With the money they received from the sales, they bought raw materials to be able to continue to work and support themselves until the next fair came around.

Merchants came from all over the country to display and sell goods. Everything could be found at these fairs: fabrics, jewelry, crafts, shoes, boots, and more. The locals put out tables with fresh bread, rolls, hot milk, tea, coffee, lemonade, ice cream, candy, and other foods and drinks. It was crowded and you could hardly move, but it was fun, and the people made enough of a profit to last them until the next big fair.

There were two main general stores in Ciechanowiec. One was owned by my father's brother and the other one was more of a bargain store. The shops were quite far from my house, but I passed them on my daily walk to school. The bargain shop was always crowded and disordered and most of the goods were damaged. In one corner of the shop, there was a barrel of shmaltz herring. When a customer would take a herring out of the barrel, the oil would spill and splatter the other merchandise with permanent stains. One could buy anything in that shop for very little money. Not far from the bargain shop was my uncle's grocery store; it was roomy, very clean, pricey, and always empty.

Each morning on my way to school, I went to the cheaper shop as I had only five *groszy* to spend. For that price, the shopkeeper would give me a piece of sausage or halva. He always gave me a generous piece that must have been worth more. I had good value for my money.

The Jewish settlement in Ciechanowiec was a "village in a village" where everyone knew everyone, or, at least, they thought they did. Ciechanowiec was quite a large shtetl and yet the closeness with which we lived our lives made it seem even smaller. People were often known by their nicknames, which were sometimes not so complimentary, but meant to be funny.

On summer Saturdays, the whole population would go to the forests for a day-long picnic. In the evenings, all the women would sit on the steps in front of the bigger houses and talk to each other about the latest romances.

My grandparents' house was on the main road, the only road to the forest. All the young lovers walked down our street together and the women on the steps looked on and gossiped. They tried to guess which couple would soon get married and who would not.

CHILDHOOD MEMORIES

During my early childhood, my family lived in one half of a two-family townhouse rented from a non-Jewish Polish family on the mostly non-Jewish side of town. I played with many non-Jewish children, spoke only Polish, and considered myself to be the same as the other non-Jewish children.

I remember when I was very young, only four years old, how I used to regularly run with the other non-Jewish children to the forest near our town to gather raspberries. We chased each other, played games, picked raspberries, and had a lot of fun.

One Saturday, my friends and I crossed the river to go to the forest. All the other children were barefoot, but I had socks and shoes on, so I took them off and left them by the river before joining the other children playing in the forest. When I returned to the river bank my shoes and socks were gone. I remember my mother's annoyance when I arrived home without my shoes that evening. My family was not well off, and it was not easy for my mother to buy a new pair of shoes. We went to the river to look for them, but we did not find them.

A teacher at the public school lived next door to us. I used to visit her very often; she talked to me and taught me the alphabet. She was beautiful and kind, and I loved her. I was eager to start learning in the school where she taught but, alas, it was not to be. My family abruptly moved to the other side of the town which was more heavily concentrated with Jewish people.

I remember waking up one morning when I was about five years old and hearing a commotion from outside where people were shouting and fighting. I looked around me; I was in my own bed, but not in my own room. I thought, *Where am I?* I remembered going to bed in my own peaceful room. Now I was in a strange place, and I didn't know why. How did I come to be there? Eventually, I understood from the conversation that my parents had to move out of their house because they couldn't afford to pay the rent. In the middle of the night, they had carried me, asleep in my bed, to our new living quarters.

The new property included the main large family home as well as a smaller home behind it. My father's sister, Brancha, who had married a man from Warsaw, operated a tailoring business in the big house at the front. The smaller house that stood in the backyard had been used as sleeping quarters for a few of my father's brothers before they were married and doubled as a workplace during the day. When this little house became empty, Brancha's husband had demanded it be signed over to him as a dowry in addition to the big house.

My father's brother, who owned the grocery store, told my mother in secret that he had received a contract to sign over the property to Brancha's husband, but he believed that this was not fair and insisted that the small house should belong to my father. Finally, after a long argument, my father's family agreed that the small house in the yard behind my paternal grandparents' big house would go to my father. We were allowed to live there rent-free.

I started to explore my new surroundings and saw that everyone lived in similar conditions. In front, on the street, were large wooden houses, the same as my grandparents' house where they lived with their married daughter and son-in-law, a tailor. There were small houses on the grounds of the large houses, so that the large, extended families could spread out and have a place to live.

In the beginning, I found it very difficult to adjust to my new neighborhood and I missed my friends so much. It took me a couple of years to settle down as I had been so happy before. For those first few years, I used to visit my old neighborhood to try to see my friends. I watched from afar the white painted home where I used to live but I was scared to walk too close.

One day, I found the courage to visit my old home, and, as I approached the front door, one of the children, a young boy named Juzik, whom I remembered well, came out of the house shouting. He yelled, "Jewess! What are you doing here?" He bent down to pick up a stone and was about to throw it at me.

Suddenly, Juzik's mother, whom I had loved so much, ran out of the house shouting, "Juzik! *Juzeuninu!* [Juzik! What are you doing!]" She hugged me, and was crying as she said, "This is our Luba!" The boy dropped the stone and bent his head in shame.

I realized then that I was not wanted and that anti-Jewish sentiments were growing. I still missed my old friends, but I started to play with my new neighbors' children. We played basketball in groups, yo-yo, and hide-and-seek. Slowly, I adjusted to my new surroundings. I never returned to my old neighborhood again as I felt unwanted and unsafe there.

MY FAMILY

My father, Jacob Wrobel, son of Shaika and Riva Wrobel, had four sisters and five brothers. All the brothers had at one stage worked for their parents without wages, but later married, left home and started their own trades.

My grandfather, Shaike Wrobel, and my father worked in partnership as wheelwrights, making wagon wheels. Every morning at dawn, my grandfather knocked at our window and called, "Wake up, Yaakov! It's time to go to work." In the main room of our house there was a long workshop table, used for making perfect, shiny wheel parts and for storing the hand tools. On hot summer days, I would watch my father work with these tools while the sweat ran down his forehead. They worked from dawn to dusk every day.

My mother Golda was very beautiful. She had dark, shiny straight hair, a pale complexion, dark eyes, a petite nose, full lips, and nice cheekbones. She was tall and slim, but seldom smiled, and always had a worried expression on her face. She was not a happy woman and was very nervous. Her life was not an easy one.

My mother moved quickly and rarely sat still. She was always busy doing something. She assisted my father in the wheelwright business during the day. During the winter nights, she knitted socks for farmers in exchange for milk. Life was difficult, as it was for many Jews in my shtetl, and my mother did all she could to help provide for her family. I recall watching her as she knitted during the night. She was quick and adept; she put the wool on four knitting needles and collected the stitches with a fifth one.

Very early in the mornings, my mother bought milk from the farmers. By the time we woke up, our breakfast, a soup made from potatoes, oats and milk, was ready to be served. During the day my mother helped my father in the business, as well as tending to all our needs. She made a Sabbath dinner every week and baked her own challah bread, rising early in the morning to do so. She also made delicious gefilte fish every week for the Friday Sabbath meal. A man would ring a bell and come down the street with a big barrel of fish and my mother would go out the street with the other women to buy the fish for the Sabbath.

In the summer, at dawn, my mother would take me to the forest to pick mushrooms and *schav*, green spinach-like leaves that grew wild in the fields. She knew where to find these and knew how to cook them because she had grown up on a farm. She also knew how to pick mushrooms and was an expert at telling the difference between the good ones and the poisonous ones.

My mother's parents, my grandmother, Hinka (née Krasnoborski), and grandfather, Gershon Tabak, had left Poland in 1890 for America. They lived in New York City for a few years. During this time some Jews left Poland to seek a better future and try their luck in the "Golden State." Their two older sons, twin boys, Pesach and Velvel, were born in America, but life was very hard there. My grandfather, who was a blacksmith by trade, could not practice his trade in the city as blacksmiths were not needed there. He could only work as a car mechanic's assistant.

When they had saved enough money, my grandparents came back to Poland and bought a farm in Sklody-Borowe, a rural area not far from Wysokie Mazowieck. Grandfather Tabak was able to run his blacksmith business once again in Poland. All the farmers from the surrounding villages came to him because he was a good tradesman and the only blacksmith in that region.

My mother, Golda Tabak, was born and raised on the farm in Sklody-Borowe, about 110 kilometers away from Ciechanowiec where she would later meet and marry my father. Aside from the older brothers, Pesach and Velvel, she also had a younger sister Pearl, and a younger brother Manes who were born in Poland.

My mother's twin brothers both served in the Polish army in World War I. Uncle Velvel was presumed dead after the war and never returned. Uncle Pesach ran a blacksmith business in Sklody-Borowe near his parents' farm. He married Sorche (Goldberg) and they had five children.

My grandparents and my uncle and his family all fled Sklody-Borowe sometime soon after 1936. During this time, antisemitism in Poland was increasing and acts of violence against Jews were becoming more common. I recall seeing Jewish stalls at the market being attacked by non-Jewish hoodlums. There were physical attacks on Jews on market days. There was antisemitic propaganda going around in Poland. Many Jewish properties were burned down during this period as an act of hate against Jews, including my grandparents' beautiful farm, the farm that they had dreamed of owning and left America for. My uncle Pesach's house and blacksmith business was also burned down, and my uncle and grandparents fled to Sokoly, a town not far from Ciechanowiec, where my Auntie Sorche's whole family lived.

In Sokoly, Uncle Pesach bought a house and workshop from Uncle Tevie. He was Sorche's uncle, a twin brother of her father. However, even though Uncle Tevie built a new house and blacksmith workshop for himself, his wife Rachel refused to move from the old house and allow Pesach to live there. There was a dreadful family feud. They called each other terrible names and Auntie Rachel took Uncle Pesach to court alleging he had assaulted her. She won the case, but my Uncle Pesach appealed to a higher court in Warsaw and hired an expensive lawyer and eventually won the appeal. My mother's younger brother Manes also moved to Sokoly where he married the sister of Sorche, Leah Goldberg.

I had two brothers; the elder, one year younger than me, was called Avraham Moshe, like my father's brother. He did not care much for religious studies and was a bit of a rebel. He was tall, dark, and handsome. He was a strong and adventurous boy and taught himself how to swim. I remember how my mother discovered him swimming in the river when he was meant to be at the *Yeshivah* studying Torah.

Each morning my mother bought fresh bread rolls from the bakery for school lunches. She always gave me a dark, cheaper roll and gave my brother a round, white, sugared roll. I always thought that she did so because she loved him more, but the real reason was that he threatened not to go to school unless he got what he wanted, and he carried out his threats.

My youngest brother, Shlomo (Solomon), was four years younger. Shlomo was very good looking, bright, and clever. He was a very articulate child with sophisticated language skills and could read the alphabet as a toddler. My father's brother who was wealthy and had no children, loved my little brother Shlomo. Each time he came to visit, he would take a book and ask Shlomo to show him the A-B-C-s. He would give Shlomo a reward for knowing the correct answers. We all loved that little boy. He was beautiful, strong, and healthy.

Shlomo had a little girlfriend from the neighborhood who was his age, and they would play together. One day, the little girl told my mother that a few weeks earlier, Shlomo had fallen into their cellar. My mother inquired further and then the girl's parents told her what happened. They had an orchard and were bringing the fruit to the big, deep cellar located at the back door of their house. Little

Shlomo, who was walking in front of them, fell into the open cellar and lost consciousness as soon as he opened the door. The girl's parents waited for him to wake up, but they were afraid to tell my parents what had happened.

After that, Shlomo complained of headaches. He became very pale and weak. We did not know what had happened to him. My mother took him to the doctor who advised sending him to a hospital in the nearby city of Bialystok. It was too late; nobody could help. Shlomo's brain and skull were damaged, but they couldn't operate, so he was brought back home. The boy suffered and our hearts ached for him. Shlomo died.

From then on, my father began ailing. He was heartbroken, and his own health deteriorated. My mother found it very difficult to run the business on her own, so she hired a young man, Vicek Dombrowski, to learn the wheelwright trade and help my father. As soon as the hired man knew the trade well enough, she paid him full wages. But he was unreliable and would drink too much on Sundays.

On Mondays, which were market days when the farmers brought wheels to be repaired, Vicek the new helper, would arrive late or not at all. My mother tried to please Vicek: she bought him ice cream; she also introduced him to a girl, a previous neighbor of ours named Janka Polonski.

Janka and Vicek had a love affair in our house, right before my eyes. Janka used to come running to see Vicek and he would accuse her of dancing with other boys and making love with them. I once saw Vicek take off his belt and whip Janka. She shouted and begged him to stop, swore she would not do it anymore; that she would behave. They made up and started kissing. They made love in a corner of the house, under the big stove.

SCHOOL YEARS

In 1930, I was five years old and attended the local public school. One day, just before the Easter holiday, I went to the dressmaker to try on a dress. I spoke only Polish, not Yiddish or Hebrew, and I crossed my heart like I saw the other Polish Christian children doing, because it was Easter. The dressmaker made a fuss and sent her daughter to call for my maternal grandmother Hinka Tabak. The dressmaker told my grandmother that they must send me to the private Jewish school, otherwise, I would grow up as a non-Jew.

And so, it came to be that I was enrolled in a private Jewish school called *Tarbut*. It was a Zionist school. The Jewish school was very far from my home, on the other side of town and I left very early each morning because I had to walk a great distance. I crossed our side of town, over two bridges and through more streets, until I reached the school.

All of the pupils were from the richest families. Only about ten percent of the Jewish children from Ciechanowiec and its surroundings attended this school. The others attended the free government schools. The Tarbut school fees were very high, but my grandmother agreed to pay them and received some financial assistance from her relations in America.

One winter morning, I woke up and the soup that my mother regularly made me before school was not ready. It was time to go to school, so I took my bag and ran away without breakfast or lunch. In the middle of the lessons, somebody knocked on the door to the classroom. The teacher asked me to go out, and there was my mother with a jug of hot soup wrapped up in a towel to keep it warm.

At that time, I didn't understand the meaning of my mother's love and that she had come all way to school because she cared about me. I remember being cross at my mother. I was so embarrassed. I made her promise never again to bring me soup, or anything else, at school.

Although I was very reluctant to attend Tarbut school at the beginning, I quickly changed my mind and was an enthusiastic student. I loved my studies and excelled in them. I was very fortunate to have such a good education. The Tarbut school had the best and most dedicated teachers. They put their heart and soul into teaching us, and in imparting important life lessons and morals. Soon, I was speaking Hebrew quite fluently. I dreamed of going to live in the land of Israel where some of the youth of Ciechanowiec had already left to work towards establishing a Jewish State. We had six lessons a day and had a different teacher for each subject. We studied Hebrew, Mathematics, Bible, History, and Geography in Polish and Hebrew. I studied a lot. I felt that I could and should be equal to all the other children and do well in my studies.

At school we studied the five books of Moses and learnt that God chose Moses to be the leader of the nation because he was the humblest of men. When the teacher explained the third book about sex, the boys in class started asking questions. The teacher talked about women's menstruation, and that under Jewish Orthodox law sex was not allowed until seven days after being clear from blood flow, and that this was for health reasons and to make sure the babies were healthy.

We also studied the books of Prophets. They taught us that the Jewish people in Biblical times had forgotten what things were important, so God sent the prophets to remind them to keep the commandments and to warn them that there would be bad consequences for disobedience. God said, "Cease to do bad, learn to do good and search for justice."

We studied all our secular subjects in the Polish language. I was the best in Polish studies because I was born into this language. We studied Polish history and learned that Jews had lived in Poland for a thousand years, since a time when Poland had been devastated by many years of war. We were taught that a clever king, Kazimierz the Great, invited Jewish refugees to live in Poland in the 16th century, because the Jews could speak many different languages and could do business with many different countries. The Jews had helped to rebuild Poland.

We also learned Jewish history, called *Korot-Evrim*. We learned that Israel was and is a Jewish country and that the Jews had wars and kings, the same as all other countries. The most famous Jewish kings were King David who was praised for his fairness, and King Solomon, who was famous for his wisdom.

I do vividly remember one unpleasant incident from those primary school years. Once a year on *Lag-Baomer,* the holiday for trees, the whole school would have a picnic in the forest. The children got free ice creams and lollies and we would sing and dance. In 1935, when we were marching to the forest for our picnic, some Polish children threw stones at us and screamed "Jews, go back to Palestine!" We felt very threatened and unsafe. We returned to school and had no more celebrations for this holiday of trees in the forest.

There were about 20 girls and 20 boys in my class. We sat on black benches – five benches on one side of the room for the girls, and five on the other side for the boys. In the middle, there was free space for the teacher to walk around. Above the benches were narrow tables. We kept our books for reading and writing on top of the tables. Below the tables were shelves for more books and our lunches. I always felt embarrassed for not having nice clothes, for not having books, and for having damaged and stained exercise books, bought for half-price from the bargain grocery store.

In my first two years at school, I had only one friend, Michelle, who was also from a working-class family. Her parents owned an old, broken-down bathhouse, where they worked and lived. Michelle's parents were always very busy heating the hot water and attending to the baths and showers, and they were too busy to take proper care of Michelle. She often came to school without lunch.

One day I saw the girls whispering in secret; I was an outsider and wasn't included in their conversations. I was then called to the school office, but I had no idea what was going on. I only noticed that my friend Michelle was not attending school anymore. I was told that she had been expelled for stealing lunches.

Suddenly, all the girls in my class were very nice to me. Before that, I sat by myself, but now they all came over and talked with me. They talked me into buying a raffle ticket and made me promise to come to the drawing of the raffle. I did go, and a girl pulled out a number and they all called out: "Luba, you won, you won!" They presented me with a beautiful blue jacquard sweater; it was the most beautiful sweater I ever owned in my whole life. I was so happy; I could not figure out my good luck.

It was only years later that I understood that this must have been a nice gesture to clear their consciences, because for a while they had suspected me of stealing their lunches. I would eat my lunches in hiding, bent over my shelf, because I was ashamed of my dark rolls when everybody else had white rolls. It must have looked very suspicious.

A few girls invited me to study with them and do our homework together at their homes, because they knew that I was a good student and didn't have my own books to study. I chose to study with Feigale Rosenblum because she lived not very far from my house.

Feigale had six brothers. The only girl in her family, she was pretty and a bit spoiled, and she didn't like to study without help. We became best friends. I practically lived in the house of the Rosenblums. After school we would walk to her family's beautiful white brick house, which was located at the edge of the forest. Feigale's father, Jacob, exported cases of eggs, butter, chickens, and cheeses by train, to be sold in Warsaw. He came home only for the weekends. The Rosenblums also had a small cheese factory. They bought their milk from Maruszewski, the landowner, and the two Rosenblum sons, along with a professional cheesemaker, made beautiful cheeses that they painted red and put in a cellar to mature.

Mrs. Rosenblum was a good-natured woman who was always working. On Mondays and Thursdays, the market days, she bought eggs and butter directly from the farmers' wagons and put them in large cases, ready to be shipped away. Since the Rosenblums lived near the forest, their house was the first stop for the farmers riding through the forest on their way to town and Mrs. Rosenblum had the first choice of their produce. On other days, she worked in the fenced-in vegetable garden near the house.

I was happy at the house of the Rosenblums. I had the best food, things I never had at home. Feigale used to pick a few eggs from the cases and throw away the whites. We ate only the yolks, mixed with sugar as a special treat. We ate as much bread, butter, and cheese as we liked. Feigale's father brought walnuts and chocolates from Warsaw, and we tasted everything. All afternoon, we would run around doing errands for Mrs. Rosenblum. In the evening, after dinner, we closed the door to Feigale's room and began to study seriously. We studied until late at night, and then one of Feigale's brothers would walk me home.

During school holidays, we played together with Feigale's dolls and toys. On nice summer days, we read books or ran to the forest to pick berries. We also watched holidaymakers. We saw students who were on holiday with Maruszewski's daughter, Dzidria, playing tennis in smart, white tennis outfits. It was a wonderful sight to watch their bodies gracefully move on the tennis court when they ran to strike the ball.

We began to grow up. We were about nine or ten years old. Feigale had beautiful clothing from Warsaw. She received a lot of presents from her relations who came to stay with them for the summer holidays. Once, I overheard one of her aunts suggest that she should look for richer girlfriends, that she should dress up in her beautiful clothing, and go on Saturdays to visit the rich girls, and not play only with Luba. We still studied together during the week, but on weekends, Feigale began to dress up and go by herself to visit the rich girls. I knew about it, but I didn't mind. I understood that I couldn't go with her because I didn't have any nice clothes.

One wintry Saturday afternoon, I was sitting in my grandmother's house looking out the window, when my grandmother pointed outside and said to me, "Look, here is Feigale all dressed up, going to town, and she never called you or looked for you. Why doesn't she call you to go with her? Is she your friend only on weekdays?"

Grandmother's words bothered me; I started feeling hurt and offended and decided not to go to Feigale's house anymore. I even stopped talking to her in school.

Mrs. Rosenblum came to my house and asked me: "Why don't you come over anymore? Have I done something wrong? Didn't I treat you right?" I told Mrs. Rosenblum that I was very happy in her house and that I loved her, but though I was grateful for everything she did for me, I wasn't going to study with Feigale anymore.

I was nine years old when I ended my friendship with Feigale, and it hurt. I missed Feigale, her good mother, her gentle brothers, the house, and the food.

I thought about improving my appearance so that I looked less shabby, and it would be easier to make friends. I started looking in the mirror and taking greater effort to brush my hair and dress neatly. I saw that I badly needed a haircut. I talked to my mother, and she arranged for me and about ten other children from the neighborhood to go together to the cheap, strange hairdresser who we called the *Katcher*.

The Katcher was a bachelor who lived alone in a house at the end of town. Each morning after breakfast, we would see him riding his bicycle, his legs bound with leather. He was tall and clean-shaven, in his forties, and was always smiling to himself. We all thought that he was not one hundred percent sane. He was very polite and spoke an educated Polish, not like ordinary people; he was originally from a big town. Once, a swagman came to him looking for work, so he gave the man a broom and asked him to clean his yard. When the man finished his work and asked for money, the Katcher refused to pay him. The man called the police, and a crowd watched the Katcher argue that the man asked for work only, so he gave him work, but the man never asked for money.

I, alongside ten other children, arrived at the Katcher hairdresser to get a haircut, as arranged. He told us to sit on a bench and gave us magazines to choose which style we liked. Then he called each one of us individually. He put us on a high, swivel chair and asked what style we would like – *Polka* or *Legason?* I could not tell one style from the other. The Katcher started cutting my hair and when I looked in the mirror, I saw that my hair had been cut very short. I came home crying. Luckily, my hair grew fast.

I began to demand new clothing, a new dress and shoes, because I wanted to be able to go out on Saturdays and holidays to visit the rich, nicely dressed schoolgirls. I kept protesting by smearing my face with black coal and crying. Finally, one evening, my mother took me to a fabric shop and bought me material for a dress. She told me that she was saving money with that shopkeeper for my dowry. That was the first time I became properly aware of the concept of dowry in our shtetl.

A JEWISH MOTHER'S WORRY

The biggest problem of the mothers in our town in Poland was saving a dowry for their daughters. From the day a girl was born, her parents started to worry about saving.

We had a neighbor who dressed up and went to town every Friday, and I was curious about where he went. My mother pointed at him and told me that he was going to a trusted merchant to save for his daughter Sarah's dowry.

In a few families, there were already some "old maids." Although they had once been very pretty, nobody would marry them without ready cash. Without money, it was impossible for a young couple to marry and make a home for themselves. They would have to live with their in-laws, who often had only one bedroom for a family of ten.

I was ten years old, and it was school holidays. It was summer, the sun was shining, and I was happy to run out early from our small house because during the daytime it was used as a workshop for my father and grandfather. I took my ball and was playing on the back wall near my grandmother's big house. Suddenly, I heard a commotion, a big rush. I looked and saw many people running, so I ran after them, and we came to the river.

On the ground under the bridge lay a 20-year-old girl who had been pulled out of the water. She had drowned. I looked at her pale, lifeless face and for the first time in my life I felt terribly distressed. I saw what had happened to such a young, beautiful girl. *What a terrible waste of a young life!* I wanted to know how and why this tragedy came about. I listened to the girl's friends and relatives talking among themselves.

The girl was an orphan; she was in love with a boy. They were going steady and were madly in love. She became pregnant and hoped that he would marry her. Instead, he left her. The girl was in great distress and her stepmother was not helpful. The shame and the gossip in a small town where everyone knew everyone else were unbearable.

The girl felt helpless, hopeless, and desperate. She was left without any aid or assistance, and she thought that death was her only solution. She had dressed up in her best outfit, with high-heeled shoes and jewelry and had put on makeup, rouge and lipstick. She looked beautiful, like a bride before her wedding. People had seen her walking up and down the bridge, looking at her watch and waiting. Her boyfriend knew what she intended to do.

She hoped that he would come and stop her; that he would not let her kill herself and the baby. Maybe he would show that he loved her, and that he cared. She waited, walked for hours, but nobody came. Everyone knew, but nobody cared. The girl decided that she had nothing and no one to live for – her shame and pain were unbearable. Nobody came to her aid, no one gave her a helping hand, and so she jumped to her death.

This girl's death had an enormous impact on me. I examined her situation again in my mind and I made a decision. I decided to remember: if this is the result of love and sex, it is not for me. No matter how much in love I may be with a man, whatever he promises, without marriage there will be no sex for me.

A few weeks later, I was playing ball again in the street when I heard a big noise. I stopped and turned around. I saw a big man running carrying a rope and shouting: "I am going to hang myself. I am going to kill myself!" His mother and sisters ran behind him, shouting: "Don't do it, please don't kill yourself!"

People gathered to look, and I heard the story. The man's family was in the butcher trade. They had three daughters and one son. All of them were tall, broad-shouldered, and red-faced, and they all were nicknamed "Oxen." The three daughters, who were in their twenties and thirties, couldn't find boyfriends. The son had a girlfriend he was madly in love with. She was pretty and had a good figure. The girlfriend wore tight skirts, low-necked blouses and high-heeled shoes. She used lipstick and rouge. The only thing she had on her mind was marriage, but she was poor, without a penny to her name.

The butcher's son bought her presents, but marriage was impossible. How could he bring her to live in his tiny, overcrowded home, when there were already four women in the house, all of them doing the housework, all of them cooking in that small kitchen?

The girl thought of a plan to make him jealous, to make him marry her without any reservations. She brought her cousin over from another town and told her boyfriend that this man had come to marry her. She agreed to cancel the wedding if the boyfriend would marry her straight away.

The butcher's son ran to announce the news to his parents and sisters about his intention to marry, but they refused to let him, so he threatened to go to the garden and hang himself. His mother and sisters took his threat seriously and ran after him, shouting: "We agree! We agree!" He turned back to them with the rope in his hand, and they all walked back home in harmony to plan the wedding.

On one of my school holidays, I visited my father's older sister, Auntie Basia Wrobel. She lived in a small town called Zareby Koscielne (Zaromb). Her husband, Jakob Wajsbord, was a good, quiet man. They had four daughters and three sons. Their only income was from commissions paid to Jakob by the local bakers and grocers for bringing them white flour from Ostrow, a town about 40 kilometers from Zareby. Traveling by horse and wagon would take Jakob about 24 hours to reach Ostrow and another 24 hours to return. They were poor, barely making a living.

All four of the Wajsbord daughters were grown. The oldest was 26 years old, the second 22, the third 20, and the youngest was 18. All of them were pretty, with good figures, but they had no money for dowries. The oldest son was 24 years old. He was tall and very handsome and looked like Gregory Peck. He had a girlfriend, but she was poor and without money; it was just a love affair.

THE HOLY MAN

One day, Auntie Basia (Wrobel) and a few other women from Zareby arrived at Grandmother's house to spend the night. They were on a journey to Sokolow to consult a clever Rabbi, a holy man, for advice. Basia told us her problem: a matchmaker had found a very good match for her handsome, good-looking son.

There was a single woman, a divorcee, who lived in the very small town of Danur (Nur) on the Bug River. The woman owned a house and a bakery. Her husband had divorced her and all the way from America he sent her 1,000 dollars. This divorcee wanted to marry Basia's oldest son. In addition, she had agreed to give dowries to Basia's two older girls who had boyfriends, so that they would be able to marry. Not only that, but the divorcee also agreed to rent an orchard with fruit trees for a season, in partnership with Jakob. The whole family could have a happy, wonderful life.

The deal offered was very generous. The problem was, should her son do it? Many members of the older generation were still very old-fashioned in their thinking. They worried about how they would be perceived. What would people say? Should he marry the divorcee, whom he didn't love? Should he leave the girl in Zareby, whom he did love and with whom he had been meeting for a couple of years?

With these questions, Basia was going to consult the holy Rabbi in Sokolow. She wanted him to make the decision and give her permission to deal with the complicated situation. It was complicated because divorce was frowned upon by the community. Basia wanted to clear her conscience and save face before the people of the town. She wanted to be able to say that the Rabbi had approved the marriage. She did not consider her son's feelings of love towards the girl in Zareby.

Basia came back from Sokolow with a letter from the Rabbi, stating that her son was granted permission to marry. The son then married the divorcee, and his two older sisters also were married. Everything was all right, for a while. The divorcee came to my grandmother's house to have her first baby. It was a breech delivery. The doctor came and turned the baby around, and the baby was delivered safely. A year later, the woman gave birth to another daughter, also by breech delivery. During the third birth, the woman died, but the baby lived. The widower took his three daughters to Zareby, where his former girlfriend was still waiting for him. She was still in love with him despite the fact that he had deserted her. He married her and she raised his children.

Auntie Basia's third daughter, Elka, came to visit Grandmother once. Elka was 20 years old. She was tall, with a slim waist, a very good figure, and a beautiful face. She had long auburn hair, green eyes, and a lovely smile. I loved to look at her. Her visit was called a "vacation" but the real reason for her coming was because she was having a love affair in Zareby with a rich boy who loved her. She wanted marriage, but the boy could not marry her unless she had money. Elka left him to make him jealous and desperate, to make him desire her so much that when she returned, he would marry her.

As soon as Elka arrived, about a dozen of her friends from a Zionist youth organization, both boys and girls, came to visit her. I was 11 years old. I watched the group of young people as the young men brought halvah, lemonade, cakes, and ice cream. They were having a party. Elka sang the latest tangos, and six pairs of slim figures danced to the tune of her singing. Elka had the most wonderful, sentimental voice. I did not leave that room until the dancing was over. I loved the songs, the romantic atmosphere, and the dancing. It made me dream and fantasize about romance and love.

My new dress was ready. I put it on along with my new shoes and combed my hair. I looked in the mirror and was satisfied with my looks. Then I walked to the other side of town, to the house of my school friend, Goldie Etkes. She was beautiful, and kind. I loved her. Everyone who knew her loved her.

On holidays, weekends, and on warm summer evenings, a whole group of boys and girls would come to Goldie's house. Together we went for walks in the park. We sat on the benches and Goldie would sing the most beautiful love songs. She had a sensual voice and all of us were happy to hear her sing more and more songs.

MY YEARS IN BIALYSTOK

In 1937, when the big market fair in Ciechanowiec was over, we knew that it had been a successful day. Father had sold a lot of wheels and barrows, and with the money from these sales, my parents went to another nearby town, Bransk, to buy more wood, the raw material for producing more wheels and barrows for the coming season. The journey by horse and wagon to Bransk and back took about four days. It was extremely cold, windy, and it was snowing. My father was already weak and sick. Since the tragic death of my younger brother he had not been the same. When they returned, father unloaded the wood, but then he collapsed. A short while later, he died.

My mother carried on the business with hired help for a time, but she was planning to find a different solution to her life. That year I finished school with distinction. I wished to study in a high school in Bialystok along with my close friend, Goldie Etkes, and about ten other girls and boys from my class. Mother explained to me that high school did not provide a way to earn an income in the future – high school was only for the wealthy.

My mother found out that some girls and boys were going to Bialystok to study at the Jewish community-funded ORT Technical

School, where trades were taught for four hours a day: dressmaking for girls, and in a separate school, carpentry for boys. During the other four hours of the school day, ORT provided studies equivalent to the end of 11th grade in high school. After three years, the students received a diploma.

Mother and I went by train to the big city, Bialystok. We came to the house of Mother's childhood friend from Sklody, Itka Buksztelsky. Mother had written ahead to let her friend know that my father had died, and I was in need of a place to stay. She explained to Itka that she would be able to manage the school fees, but she would not be able to pay for room and board. Itka told her not to worry, that I could stay at her place without charge and that I would be treated as her own daughter.

I was accepted at the ORT Technical School and started my first year. At the beginning, we were taught how to take measurements and make patterns from fashion magazines, and how to recognize the quality of materials. We also went to factories to learn, and watched how fabrics were made. We sewed by hand, using different kinds of stitches. To obtain the best results, the teacher was extremely strict and demanded only perfection. In the second and third years, we sewed by machine. We learned how to cut material, how to prepare a dress for fittings, and how to produce a finished garment. At the end of the third year, there were exams, and I received a diploma. It was a very good school. I received an excellent education.

On weekends, the boys and girls from our town would meet at the boarding house where a few of our girls were staying. We discussed the events of the week and went for walks in groups on the main streets. My friend, Golda Etkes, was staying with a Bialystok family; I used to visit her often. We went to the cinema and when there was a musical, Goldie picked up the nicest songs and later sang them to the group.

Occasionally, Goldie and the other girls came to visit me at Itka's place, where I was staying. It was a nice apartment in a big building. It had a large kitchen with water and electricity, a very large dining room but only two bedrooms.

Itka's youngest son, Matis, was a student. He was 15 years old, tall, and very handsome. When the girls saw him, they fell in love with him and were jealous that I lived in the same apartment with such a handsome young man. In the beginning, I thought so too, but gradually, after I saw how he treated Joheved, Itka's niece, who had a disability, I stopped liking him. I looked at Matis and I didn't see his beauty anymore. I saw only his unattractive, spoiled behavior.

Joheved was Matis's cousin, the daughter of his mother's sister. Itka's sister, her husband and five children, had all gone to America. Joheved, who was then 20 years old, was left behind. She was rejected by the American Immigration Authority because she was disabled and had the mental age of a six-year-old. Itka, her kind aunt, agreed to take her in.

When I came to live with Itka in 1937, Joheved was already 35 years old. She did all the odd jobs in the house: she washed the floor, peeled potatoes, and collected groceries from the shop with a list. She could not speak properly, but after a while I understood her unique dialect and I grew to like her very much.

I watched how Matis treated Joheved. He would stand near the sink and call out to Joheved to bring him a glass of water. When Joheved was busy in the bedroom, she would help Matis take off his boots, and he would deliberately kick her. I learned that no matter how good-looking a man is on the outside, his looks are of little importance. I saw that lasting beauty is inside a person and stopped admiring Matis's good looks. I saw only a spoiled brat who had no consideration for others. I understood then that for a lasting relationship, the most important thing is a man's nature, his behavior, how he treats people, and how he cares.

Itka treated me like her own daughter. She was a good, kind-hearted woman. She had a family of four sons, one daughter, and four grandchildren. All her children were good-natured, but Matis, the youngest, was very spoiled. Three of Itka's children were married. I would have meals with them a few days a week and on Saturday nights, they would take me to the theater and afterwards to the ice cream parlour.

On lonely winter nights, Itka and I would sit down together to play cards and she would tell me stories from her life. When Itka was young and living in Sklody she fell in love with a boy. She gave him her dowry money so that he would be able to go to America instead of joining the army. He left for America, and she never heard from him again. After that, Itka went to Bialystok to find work. There, she met her husband Szmulke and he fell in love with her. He was not good-looking, but he was rich. At first, she refused to marry him, so he went to her father and offered money for a dowry. Itka's father came and told her to marry Szmulke, so she did. In front of her family, Itka would complain that she still didn't love her husband, but he used to smile and say, "I have the best-looking woman in Bialystok."

Itka was a woman of spirituality. She knew how to tell fortunes by examining tea leaves, something she must have learned in her childhood in Sklody. Many women came to see her to have their fortunes told. Others came for advice and help. Her generosity was unlimited.

I remember when my auntie Sorche had come crying to her when they first came to live in Sokoly because they could not afford to pay for the expensive legal fees in the court case with Uncle Tevie and Itka had given Sorche a few hundred *zlotys*. I watched her assist many people that came to her for help.

One evening, Mrs. Hepner, the lady who owned the grocery store, came into Itka's apartment, and told her that she went bankrupt. She had used up all the money from her store. She had run out of merchandise and was unable to buy new stock. Her eldest daughter was about to be married and Mrs. Hepner was worried that if the groom found out that she had no money, he would decide to cancel the wedding. Itka asked her how much money she needed, then took a money bag out of her bosom and gave Mrs. Hepner a few hundred zlotys. Mrs. Hepner asked how she would repay her, but Itka told Mrs. Hepner not to worry, and that the money was a gift.

THE NAZI INVASION OF POLAND
OUTBREAK OF WORLD WAR II: 1939

In 1939, I finished school, received a diploma, and came back home to Ciechanowiec. I was nervous about coming home as so many things had changed since I left. While I was living and studying in Bialystok, my mother had remarried. Her new husband, Chaim Kawka, was a widower from Czyzewo, a nearby town. My mother had borne another child, Shmuel, a handsome little boy. My stepfather was very happy to have a son because he only had three daughters from his previous marriage. My 13-year-old brother, Avraham Moshe, was sent away to study at a yeshiva in the town of Siemiatycze whilst I was in Bialystok, but he soon arrived back in Ciechanowiec.

Back in Ciechanowiec, I felt tension in the air. People were sitting motionless by their radios, listening to the war reports. They already knew that on March 13, 1938, German troops had entered Austria and annexed Germany's neighbor, Hitler's native land, into the German Reich.

In September 1938, Prime Minister Neville Chamberlain of Great Britain and Edouard Daladier of France entered into the Munich Agreement with Hitler, which supposedly guaranteed peace in return for Britain and France not opposing Germany's occupation of the Sudetenland area of Czechoslovakia. Six months later, in defiance of that Agreement, German troops occupied the remainder of Czechoslovakia. On May 22, 1939, Mussolini signed a pact with Hitler, each of them committing his nation to join the other in war. On August 23, 1939, Stalin signed a non-aggression pact with Germany.

In the early hours of September 1, 1939, German tanks rolled, the guns roared, and Hitler's *Wehrmacht* stormed across Poland's borders. It was the birth of the Blitzkrieg, and the death of freedom. There was a glimmer of hope when Great Britain and France declared war on the Third Reich, but by then, the Nazi panzer divisions were well into Poland and the *Luftwaffe* controlled the skies. Polish resistance crumbled against the mechanized might of the German armies.

My mother dug a hole in the ground behind our house, in which she put most of our belongings. That evening, we all went to hide in our neighbor's big cellar. I looked out of the cellar's tiny window and saw German soldiers. They were shouting, with such wild voices that I shivered at the sound of them. We stayed in that cellar all night and then, in the morning, each family went back home.

In the morning, German soldiers were patrolling the streets. Young Polish hoodlums walked with the Germans, pointing out Jewish houses and shops. The German soldiers seized old Jewish men for forced labor and beat them. They broke into shops and houses, raping girls and women. The German soldiers, together with the Polish hoodlums, carried out acts of violence with the utmost brutality.

UNDER RUSSIAN OCCUPATION

I was lucky to miss a lot of suffering. A well respected, wealthy Polish farmer came to my mother to request that all teenagers from our neighborhood come to his farm to dig potatoes. In return, he promised to pay for the work, with potatoes. I went together with about 20 others.

We were digging potatoes, when suddenly we heard an unusual noise. We stood up and saw large Russian tanks rolling over the fields. Stunned, I looked at the barrel of the gun on a tank. The soldiers inside the tank were turning the gun barrel round and round. When I looked behind me, I saw groups of Polish soldiers in uniforms, holding bicycles and running in the field. The Russians in the tanks saw the running soldiers, but they were reluctant to shoot, because they also saw all of us young teenagers in the same field. The Polish soldiers got safely away. After a few more days, we finished the work at the farm and returned home to find that the Russians were already in town. We were glad because they liberated us from the brutal, German Nazis.

My mother's older brothers – the twins – had served in the Polish army during World War I. After the war, only Pesach returned to Ciechanowiec, Velvel did not; he was presumed dead. The border between Poland and Russia was closed until the start of World War II in 1939. Suddenly, one day, my Uncle Velvel, whom we presumed had been killed in action in the first war, appeared. My grandfather had already passed away, but my grandmother Hinka Tabak was still alive.

My poor grandmother Hinka fainted from shock when she saw Velvel was alive. Velvel said he had not been allowed to come back to Poland from Russia and had settled in Yekaterinoslav where he had married a Russian woman, had children, and worked as a blacksmith. My grandmother was overjoyed to see him, even only briefly, before he returned over the border.

All the families who lived in bigger houses had to take in and share their homes with a Russian family. Some of these were the families of Russian officers; some were civilians. A Russian family lived next door to us. The father was a director at the tax office and when he asked my mother why I was not working, she showed him my certificates and diploma and told him that the reason I was unable to work was because I did not speak Russian. The director told my mother that he had received an order to send a local girl to Novogrudok to study Russian for three months. He offered to send me, and said that after I returned, I would be able to work in his office.

When I arrived in Novogrudok, I shared a room with three other girls. We were given good food at a restaurant close to the school. There were 300 students from all over Poland. The teacher gave us lessons and homework. When he called me to the front of the class, I explained that I didn't understand the lesson in Russian, which annoyed him. But I was determined to study hard and to succeed and the three girls with whom I shared the room spoke only Russian, so, very soon, I spoke the language like a native.

Once, in an accounting lesson, the teacher made jokes about accountants in Russia; how they put "debit" on one side in the account books, "credit" on the other, and the profit in their pockets. I wrote out the whole lesson, each word with Polish and

Russian texts, and memorized it all. The next time I was called to the front of the class, I was able to explain the whole lesson in perfect Russian. This time the teacher was pleased; he even praised me in his other classes and advised students to come and study with me.

Two students began to come to our place each morning to study with me. Then there was only one, Wolodka. He was tall, pleasant, and good-looking. I was 16 years old, and he was 21. We studied and had conversations; we sat close and talked to each other, I felt his closeness. My body was awakening and for the first time in my life, I was in love. I knew that nothing could come of it, but I was so happy to see him, to sit close to him, to look in his eyes, to hear his voice.

One evening, Wolodka came to see me. He was very restless; he didn't sit down, but just walked up and down the room. When I asked what was wrong, he said that he had a room by himself and wished me to move in with him. I could see that he meant it, that he was serious. He said we could register as husband and wife; a lot of students from his class were doing that; it was very popular. He gave me three days to think it over. Since the Russians had come to Poland, all moral values had changed. Even in my town, respectable girls were freely walking with Russian officers, some even married them. I felt tempted, but I knew that for me it was impossible. I could not bring a stranger, a non-Jew, into our home, to my stepfather. Our neighbors and relations were clinging so strongly to the old traditions that for me to intermarry would be the greatest shame for the whole family.

For three days Wolodka didn't show up. I missed him terribly, but I knew that my answer would be no. On the third evening, Wolodka came and asked about my decision. I told him that it was impossible. He left and never came back, not even to study. I felt hurt, lonely, and sad, but I knew that I had made the right decision. One day, I saw Wolodka waiting outside my classroom for a Russian girl named Zina Margunov. She came out and they left together. I was jealous and heartbroken, but I told no one about my pain and suffered alone for the rest of my degree.

School was over and I received a diploma. On the way back to my town, I traveled by train to Bialystok. At the Bialystok station, I saw Wolodka all alone, waiting with his luggage. He was pale and very nervous, so I walked up to him, and he told me his problem: he had married Zina in the registry office, but she had never told him, until just now, in the train station, that she had been sharing her apartment in Bialystok with a man and that he was still living there. She told Wolodka to wait in the station and went ahead to her apartment to try to get rid of her former boyfriend. She said that if she succeeded, she would come back to get him. Wolodka was so broken-hearted and unhappy that I felt sorry for him. But I was also relieved; I was free, with no problems of my own. I was glad that I didn't have a husband and so many worries.

After the Russians took over, the economic situation worsened from day to day. The local stores had to close because of the high taxes that were imposed on them. In the government shops, everything was scarce, and the quotas for the goods on hand were outrageous. Some tradesmen worked in cooperatives, but their wages were very low. On the black market, everything was very expensive.

In the primary schools, the Russian teachers would preach anti-religious philosophy during the time that had previously been devoted to teaching religion. The regular sports activities stopped, and all the heated discussions stopped as people were too scared to argue freely. Every so often, people would remind each other that one must hold their tongue. A few cross, unhappy men became informers. We knew of one hot-tempered, illiterate, old Jewish man and one Polish communist who came back from jail. They gave the Russian authorities the names of a few Polish and Jewish boys who belonged to the *Bund* Labor Party or the *Beitar* Zionist Party.

In the middle of the night, the Russians came to arrest these boys, but they had outsmarted the authorities and fled over the border.

The Russians then arrested their entire families, including whoever happened to be living in each house, whether they were relatives or strangers, and sent them all to Siberia. In Russia they did not have a law that each person is an individual and is not responsible for others. As a result, many innocent people suffered.

All the young boys were conscripted and sent to working battalions stationed in Osoviec-Grajewo on the German border, where they were put to work building fortifications. The working conditions were appalling. They worked from dawn to dark, with very little food. My brother Avraham Moshe (Wrobel) returned from working in Osoviec with a bill for food, because according to the officials, the wages for digging and building didn't cover the cost of the food. My mother had to pay the difference.

I had returned from my studies and started working in the RAIFO, the Russian taxation office. I worked under a Russian girl named Dusia Kaycruk. She was 25 years old, intelligent, and she was very good to me. All we had to do was receive invoices and reports from the accountants for the cooperatives.

We had to summarize these and then send a report to the government, along with an account regarding the amount of taxes that all the cooperatives had paid for that month. Every month, we sent this report to the head office in Bialystok. The rest of the month we sat in the office and did practically nothing. All that Dusia did was make a few telephone calls, but I was amazed at the big report she had written to the head office about the huge amount of work she had done throughout the month, when, in reality, we sat and talked most of the day.

Dusia used to tell me her dreams; she wanted to dress to improve her looks and figure, to find a lover. She lived in a room with two other girls from Russia, one of which used makeup, dressed nicely, and had a lot of admirers. She came from Russia with very old-fashioned clothing. Her coat was too long and too wide, her boots were wide and flat-heeled. She looked shabby and dreamed that when summer came, she would dress smartly. She would force the shoemakers' cooperative to make her shoes and boots with high heels.

Dusia had the authority to check the accountants. She sent me to the accountant from the shoemakers' cooperative to check his books and I sat there for a whole day to go over the books with the invoices. Something didn't add up, so I went and gave the figures to Dusia who went to the cooperative and came back with a new pair of boots. Dusia didn't send me to the accountant from the food cooperative. She said that she knew him well and received food parcels from him. In the invoices from the food cooperatives, I saw that 90 percent of the cost of bread and alcohol went to the tax department and only ten percent was paid to the farmers and bakers.

A Polish girl worked at the same office, in another room. She was very beautiful. A Russian man named Paddubin liked her. She told us that he made advances towards her; he wanted her to have sex with him. He was the boss in her office, but she didn't like him. She told him that she was religious, that she went to church and loved and respected the priest.

One day, the priest came to beg the girl's boss to lower the taxes paid by his church. Instead, the girl's boss imposed such a huge tax on the church that the priest was unable to pay and was forced to close the church. Paddubin laughed at the priest and was mean to him. The Polish girl sided with the priest; she pleaded and spoke harshly to Paddubin. After that, we didn't see her at work. When we asked the other Polish girls what happened to her, and why she was not at work, they told us that she and her whole family had been arrested during the night. They were sent to Siberia.

I gave all my wages to my mother and stepfather. I was happy that I was able to help them and that I was no longer a burden to my family. Despite the hard conditions, most people were happy under the Russian regime, because the whole population had equal rights.

THE GERMANS RETURN

It was Sunday, June 22, 1941. We were awakened at five o'clock in the morning, by the loud sound of airplanes. I got dressed and went out in front of the house, together with my brother Avraham Moshe (Wrobel) and my two-year-old stepbrother Shmuel (Kawka). We wondered what all the commotion and noise was about and wanted to find out.

All our neighbors and their children, as well as some Russian officers, were outside, looking into the sky and watching as the airplanes quickly and frequently came and went with white clouds forming behind them. The Russian officers told us that it must be the Russian air force on maneuvers, but when we heard bombardments very close by, we soon realized that this was a German attack. As we later found out, most of the Soviet Air Force fell victim to the total lack of preparedness of their armed forces. Soviet aircrafts were destroyed on the ground by German bombs on the first day of that battle.

We should have already packed our possessions, but my mother had left a few days before the bombing to go to the dentist in Bialystok and we were unprepared. While we were standing and looking at the sky, my stepfather angrily came out, shouting at us to come back inside. We had to start packing and hide all our personal possessions. That's when we heard a loud crash and explosion; our house shook, and we fell to the ground. We left all our belongings and parcels in the middle of the room and rushed outside to find out what happened.

My eyes saw what no one should witness: all the neighbors and their children, who had been standing together with us no more than five minutes earlier, healthy, and alive, were all either dead or badly wounded. It was a massacre, the wounded were bleeding, moaning, and gurgling. I was shocked and numb. I saw Rosa Roshatzki's 16-year-old only daughter lying dead on the ground, and her mother shaking and calling her. I saw my auntie Basia Wrobel's four boys, all of them dead. I remembered Basia holding the youngest, a one-year-old boy, dancing with him and singing and telling me, "I am the richest woman. I have four beautiful boys, who will get four dowries."

I saw Hana-Beila, the only daughter of Velvel the shoemaker. She had just been married three months ago and her wedding had been such a happy occasion for everyone. Now, Hana-Beila was lying on the ground. One of her legs was blown off and her blood was flowing. She lived in the city and had just stopped at her parents' house to collect some items when she was hit. I watched Hana Beila's husband, Josl Jarmuse's son as he tried to lift his wife and carry her over his shoulder. I heard a deafening scream from Hana-Beila.

We did not return to our house to retrieve our possessions. Instead, we ran to the forest, to the fields, far away from destruction and violent death. Hundreds of people ran with us. We stayed all day in the forest and in the evening, we headed back home. When we reached what had been our family's house, we found only a chimney. We were left without a home, without spare clothing, without beds, and without food. We had absolutely nothing, only what we wore on our bodies.

In the meantime, my mother had returned from Bialystok. She had been sure that all of us were dead, killed in the attack, and she cried with relief when she found us alive. I expected a scene because we had not hidden our possessions, but to my delight, Mother didn't mind at all. She didn't even ask us about our things. She only asked if we were hungry and ran to get food for us from her Polish friends.

The vast majority of the wooden houses on our side of town were destroyed and burned. Most of the population took shelter in the remaining houses. It was very crowded. We saw automobiles carrying remnants of the retreating Soviet Army, running away to the Russian border. Officials and their families also tried to escape but the roads were crowded. German bombs had killed nearly all the people on the roads.

I looked through the window and saw German panzer divisions on the main road. This was the biggest mechanized army in the world. It ran day after day, without stopping. Hitler's instructions to his army were "to regard the civilian population as sub-human and unfit to live." This order was taken literally by many of the German soldiers, some of whom were not even members of the SS. They tortured and killed many, many civilians.

My mother decided that it would be best for me to go and stay with her younger sister, Auntie Pearl, in Wysokie-Mazowieckie for a while. She took me to the main road, where a group of people was ready to travel to Wysokie. When I said goodbye, I looked into my mother's eyes, and they were full of sadness; maybe she knew that I would never see her again. I did not understand that then. I certainly had no idea it would be the last time I ever saw my mother or my brother or my grandmother. I will never forget that sad look in my mother's eyes for as long as I live.

I followed the others who were on their way to Wysokie-Mazowieckie. It housed all the government offices of the neighboring villages and towns. Half of the town was part of Wysokie Powiat and belonged to my hometown Ciechanowiec. The other half belonged to Bielsk Podlaskier Powiat. It was 20 kilometers away from Ciechanowiec.

Before the war broke out, there was a daily shuttle service from Ciechanowiec to Wysokie and back. A man operated this shuttle service with a horse and wagon. I recall visiting my Auntie Pearl for the school holidays when I was about nine years old. We traveled through forests and villages. There were no proper roads, and the ride was very bumpy. The driver slept all night and the horse navigated through the terrain. The horse knew the way because he had been taking the same route for so many years.

During my stay with Auntie Pearl when I was a young girl, I enjoyed beautiful food and beautiful cakes baked by Pearl. I saw my Uncle Rotkowski drink the strongest vodka with his Polish friend, the chemist, but they said it never affected their health, supposedly because they ate fried pig fat after they drank! Rotkowski always looked so stern and strict that I was afraid even just to look at him at the beginning of my stay. I kept out of his way. He must have known I was a bit scared of him because he tried to make an effort with me; he smiled and tried to talk to me, but I was shy.

I remembered that one day a circus came to Wysokie. The circus performers came to Rotkowski to get haircuts and in return, they gave the whole family free tickets to the circus. Rotkowski took me and his four younger children to the circus! He walked ahead and the five of us followed. I saw a different man, I saw a nice, proud father who bought us ice cream and lollies. He smiled and he was not a frightening person anymore.

As I traveled once again to my auntie's home, I recollected the story told to me by my mother's mother, Grandmother Hinka Tabak, about how her younger daughter, Pearl, was married in 1918, at the end of World War I, when Poland was occupied by Germany. Abraham Rutkowski lived in Wysokie with his beautiful wife and six-month-old baby boy. His wife fell in love with a good-looking German officer and left her husband and baby to run away with him. Abraham found out that the officer had been transferred to

Zambrow and found the house the officer lived in with his wife. When only the housekeeper was home, he went into the house. The housekeeper gave him a photo in which his wife was embracing the officer. He showed it to the Rabbi of Wysokie and got a divorce.

My auntie Pearl was 18 years old when she came from the farm in Sklody to Wysokie on a market day. She was good-looking and very clever. Abraham Rotkowski saw her and liked her instantly. Shortly after that, they were married. Rotkowski was tall and handsome, a very presentable person. He was educated and treated people with minor illnesses. He was also a hairdresser and made a good living. Pearl and her husband were comparatively wealthy, because they had a large house and a hairdressing salon in the center of the city.

Though they were sisters, Pearl did not look like my mother. My mother was tall and thin; Pearl was plumpish and well-groomed. She had five children, including her husband's oldest son. When World War I ended, the German officer left Rotkowski's first wife and she came to see her son, who was already grown up, but he was not interested; he was happy to regard Pearl as his mother.

Aside from her son from the previous marriage, Pearl had other children: a 12-year-old son and three daughters: Toiba, who was a year older than me; Judith, who was a year younger than me; and the youngest, Devora, who was five years old. The children were nice-looking and quiet, and never misbehaved. If they tried to disagree, one look from their father was enough to keep them in line.

In 1941, I was back again at Auntie Pearl's house, this time under vastly different circumstances. In 1939, when the Germans first occupied Poland, they burned down all Wysokie, including Pearl's beautiful house. The family had started to rebuild, but only one room was ready, and it was crowded. The entire family and I slept on the floor. We had to clean up the room very early in the morning, because it was used as a hairdressing shop during the day.

Young people, friends of Pearl's older son, would often sit and discuss the sad situation and their hopelessness and despair. Dozens of decrees had been passed against the Jews. A ghetto was established with barbed wire around it and there was a death penalty for any Jew found outside the ghetto.

LIFE IN SOKOLY GHETTO

One day, my two uncles from Sokoly, my mother's brothers, Pesach, and Manes (Tabak) arrived at Pearl's house. They were doing forced labor for the Germans, near Wysokie. There had been an accident at work, and they were let off early. They suggested that I come home with them to Sokoly, and I agreed.

On the way to Sokoly, my Uncle Pesach told me that the situation in Sokoly was slightly better than it was in other towns, and that this was thanks to a man named Marshalek. During the Russian occupation of Poland, Marshalek lived with his wife and children in a hut at the edge of the forest, just outside Sokoly. He had long hair and a beard and spent his time going begging from village to village.

My aunt's cousin, Moshe Maik, was a radio mechanic. Marshalek used to bring a hidden radio to Moshe for repair and Moshe was such a nice person that he never charged the beggar for his work. Marshalek liked Moshe. He also knew most of the Jews of Sokoly to be hard-working, honest people. Now, when the Germans occupied Sokoly, Marshalek suddenly became the boss of the town. He shaved off his beard, dressed in a German uniform and became the town's mayor. During his period of authority, the Jews of Sokoly were protected from the terror that afflicted other neighboring towns, such as Tiktin (Tykocin) and Rudki. However, fear and the death penalty always hovered in the background.

Ninety percent of the men of Sokoly were forced to work in nearby Lapy, in the railroad workshops. Each morning, they traveled to work by train. They loaded and unloaded very heavy shipments from arriving and departing trains, and repaired those trains that were out of order. Many of these workers were crushed underneath heavy loads or were beaten to death by the German guards. The other ten percent of the men worked for the German police in Sokoly.

A few days a week, Uncle Pesach would hire a replacement for his job in Lapy, so he could work in his blacksmith shop. In exchange for his work, Pesach received food from the farmers. Pesach's wife, Sorche, owned a cow. Every morning at four o'clock, two of their children would take the cow to the pasture. Sorche sold some of the milk and other food items and scrimped on food for her own family. She kept reminding us that she had to save money for the dowries of three teenaged daughters.

Then one day, the German administration ordered the Jews to turn all their cows over to the Germans. Ninety cows, owned by Jews with grieving hearts were brought to the Germans. Several people did not give up their cows and took the chance that they could get away with it. Unfortunately, they found that they were in terrible trouble. This was the case with my Uncle Pesach Tabak, the blacksmith. Because he had a family of five children, he decided not to give up his cow to the Germans, but rather to take it to one of his friends, a gentile. However, someone informed on him, and he was severely beaten by the Germans. He also had to pay a large fine. The cow, of course, was taken away from him.

One early morning, Sorche, her three daughters and I went to the Mazury Forest to pick raspberries. The forest was about eight kilometers away from Sokoly, exactly halfway to Wysokie. We were picking buckets full of raspberries near the main road when we saw Sorche's younger sister, Liba, who lived in Wysokie, walking alone to Sokoly; she was pregnant and showing. When we asked Liba why she undertook such a long journey on foot – it was 16 kilometers to Sokoly – she explained that she had heard that her youngest brother, Chaim, was sick, and she was going to visit him. I later learned the truth. Liba had a problem, a secret that she couldn't send with anyone else; she had to come by herself. Liba went to her sister Lea to tell her what weighed heavily on her mind.

Liba's husband, Josef (Kavior) the tailor, was very handsome. Liba loved him and was pregnant with her first baby. To provide food for his wife, and also for his mother and sister, Josef took his sewing machine and traveled around among the farms and villages. In return, he received food. He was on the road all week, and on the weekends, he brought home food for his whole family.

One day, Cousin Myrka arrived from Ciechanowiec to stay with Liba. Myrka was 25 years old, pretty, and had a good figure. She knew how to sew and offered to help Liba's husband. She went traveling with Josef for a whole week, but when they came back home for the Sabbath, Liba noticed that something was going on between her husband and Myrka. She saw the way he stole glances in Myrka's direction and how she pretended not to notice. When Liba was in the next room, she saw them kissing; she understood that Myrka was a threat to her marriage and that she was trying to steal her husband. The only solution was to send Myrka to Sokoly, to Liba's sister, Lea. Lea agreed to help, and Myrka was sent to Sokoly.

After the cow was taken away from Auntie Sorche, food became even scarcer. I was feeling useless and wanted to help. Luckily, Uncle Manes came. He asked me to come live with his family and help Lea with his two children, because he was forced by the Germans to go every day to work in Lapy. Lea, who was pregnant, resented her husband's never being at home to help her. He had to leave the house early at dawn and returned only late at night.

Lea demanded from her husband and me that we should be as active and hard-working as she was herself. A few times a week, Lea and I would go to the forest to gather wood for the fire to heat the house. I carried very heavy bags of wood for about three kilometers; it was a back-breaking load. Some nights, Manes and I went to a hidden oil factory, where we pressed oil from seeds with a hand machine. It took a whole night to squeeze out a few liters of oil. I had to obey every order Lea gave me, no matter how hard or dangerous it was, because I needed a place to stay. Lea compensated in other ways, by letting me wear all her best dresses and shoes.

In the middle of one night, in winter of 1942, Lea felt birth pains and woke me up. She told me to get dressed and go get the midwife, who lived on the other side of the street, opposite the German police station. It was forbidden to walk outside at night, and the penalty for doing so was death. I knew how dangerous it was, but I had to go, so I did as I was told. On the way, I prayed that God would protect me.

I returned safely with the midwife. We had a surprise; twins were born, a boy, Shlomo and a girl, Hinda. They were very beautiful babies: the boy, a redhead, was bigger; the girl was blonde with blue eyes, very delicate, but healthy. It was an exceptionally cold winter, and we needed a lot of supplies for the twins.

I did not have an easy time looking after the twins. I think they were sensitive to the atmosphere around them, and it made them insecure. When they cried together, it was deafening. When one of them would start to scream in the middle of the night, the other would wake up too. I would jump in panic out of my bed to warm their bottles of milk.

One day, Lea saw that Poles were standing in a queue on the main street and that they were receiving sugar from the German administration. She came in, in a rush, and ordered me to go out and stand in the queue. I knew that this idea was useless and very dangerous, that the only thing I could get from the Germans was not sugar, but a severe beating. Yet I obeyed. I stood in that queue with the yellow badges of the Star of David sewed onto the back and front of my coat. The Polish people looked at me in wonder with questions in their eyes, but they never said a word. I was the only Jewess who dared to stand there.

The German *Amtskommissar* [civilian administrator], who had a fearsome reputation, came over to me and asked what I was doing there. I told him that my auntie had given birth to twins and that she needed sugar for the babies. He was surprisingly sympathetic and answered nicely that he was sorry, but there was no sugar for Jews. I left and went back home without the sugar.

The Germans issued an order that all the houses around their quarters were to be demolished and Lea's house was one of them. It was a very large, two-storied house. A lot of wood was lying around in the yard behind the police station. One freezing morning at daybreak, Auntie Lea told me to pick up a few pieces of wood and put them in her shed. We both looked around; we saw nobody, and thought it was safe. The day before, a German policeman had waved a gun and shouted a warning that whoever took a piece of this wood would be shot. I knew we shouldn't touch the wood; it was dangerous. But Lea said, "It's winter, we must keep warm. It's for the twins, so take it." She opened the door of the shed.

Around midday, I was doing housework and had forgotten all about the wood. The twins had been fed and changed, I was peeling potatoes, when suddenly the door opened with a bang and a tall German policeman with a wire spring whip in his palm stood there, beckoning with his finger, saying, "Come, come." I felt trapped, numb with fear.

I looked at the whip and I heard him say: "Where are the four pieces of wood that you took?" I looked at Lea who turned her head and blinked her eyes to say nothing, so I didn't answer. But the German kept on talking: "I saw you, you in that blue sweater. I looked from the attic window. You picked up four pieces of wood. Where are they?"

Lea brought the keys from the shed and I put the wood back in the yard. I looked at the wire spring whip. I was sure that I was going to get a beating and was surprised when he didn't even touch me. He just looked at me, then turned around and said, "Bring 400 Russian rubles to our office by 12 o'clock tomorrow, or you will be shot." Then he left.

I went into the house and asked Lea if she could give me 400 rubles. She said no and didn't even seem to care much. I was worried and thought, *What can I do?' I could run away, but where would I go? Who needs me? I am needed here, but if I do not produce the money, I will be shot.* I remembered that, when I left Ciechanowiec, my mother had pushed some rubles into my hand, but I had refused to take them. I was not interested in any money, at that time, especially Russian money.

I looked through the window and I saw the *Kommandant* [Chief] of the police station in the yard, talking to Mr. Chaim Yehoshua Olsha, a member of the *Judenrat* (Jewish Council). I approached them, excused myself for interrupting them and told them my problem. I said, "I took four pieces of wood for my Auntie. I have to pay 400 rubles by 12 o'clock and I don't have my own money. My auntie doesn't care enough to pay. What shall I do?"

The Kommandant said, "Go and tell your auntie that if she doesn't give you the money, we will confiscate her belongings." I told Lea what was said, upon which she immediately produced 400 rubles and gave them to me. I took the money to the office of the police station and was given a receipt. The matter was closed; it was never mentioned again.

Lea came to an arrangement with a farmer; she gave him some household goods and he agreed to give her milk for the twins. We had to collect the milk ourselves, and the only way to do this was to sneak out of the ghetto. Although the ghetto in Sokoly was not fenced off, it was patrolled, and a strict curfew was in place. I was chosen to be the milk collector for our family; every morning at daybreak I put on my coat inside-out, so that the yellow Star of

David tags were hidden and walked to the village of Bruszewo, about four and a half kilometers away, to collect milk for the twins. It was a dangerous walk; I was playing with fire. Jews were not allowed to go out of town, curfew time was very early with a death penalty for not obeying the order. It was forbidden to carry any food.

I walked to the village of Bruszewo and back each morning. For a time, nobody saw me, I was lucky. Then, one morning, when I was on my way back to town with the milk, death stared me in the face. It was still dark when I saw the German Amtskommissar with four of his policemen, walking away from town on a hunting expedition with their dogs and rifles on their shoulders. I was walking on the edge of the road from the village to the town. The Germans were walking toward me in the middle of the road, on their way to the forest. The encounter was sudden and unexpected. I was very exposed, at the mercy of those Germans. My first impulse was to run. Then I felt as if a switch was turned on inside my brain, telling me: "Don't panic; don't run." I forced myself to calm down.

Instead of running away, I turned from my path and moved slowly to the middle of the road, towards the Germans. In a cheerful voice, I greeted them with a "Good morning." They all answered, "Good morning," and let me go on my way. They didn't even stop me or ask any questions.

Early in the morning of the next day, during curfew hours, a man walked outside the town carrying food for his family. His name was Dov Berel Krushevsky. When he saw the Germans, he panicked and ran but the Germans caught and arrested him. The next day, they hanged him in the middle of Sokoly. Dov Berel's wife and children, and all the Sokoly people, including me, were forced to watch the hanging. The Germans left him hanging for three days, so that on Sunday, when the farmers came to church, they would also see the man hanging from the gallows.

At my Auntie Lea's house, I had to do all the hard work. Cousin Myrka slept late and never did anything to help. When I asked my

Auntie about it, she told me that she had promised her sister Liba that she would keep Myrka in Sokoly at any cost. When Myrka was unhappy, she threatened to go back to Wysokie, so we all had to be nice to her.

Myrka came from the same town as I did, from Ciechanowiec, where she had a mother, three younger sisters, and a brother. She told us that she had a boyfriend at home, who was very poor, like herself. He went to work at a *Hachshara* farm, where young boys and girls were preparing for immigration to Mandate of Palestine. They worked on the farm for a couple of years, after which they received a certificate to immigrate. Myrka's boyfriend left for Mandate of Palestine.

In the meantime, Myrka went to Lodz, a large industrial town near Bielsk, to work in a fabric factory. When her boyfriend in the Mandate of Palestine sent her an immigration permit, she refused to leave Lodz, because she was having a love affair with the boss's son. She hoped to marry the boy, but it was only a dream; he did not intend to marry her.

Then the war broke out and Myrka returned home. Her family's house was burned down in 1941, and that was when she came to Wysokie. In Sokoly there was very little food to buy. The limited amount of food that was available was very expensive. Lea received a letter from Liba, telling her that food was a lot cheaper in the Wysokie ghetto, especially oil and meat. She decided to send me to Wysokie to buy meat and oil.

I was to go to Wysokie together with another girl, Dina Krasnoborski. Dina was originally from Wysokie. She had a sick mother and an 11-year-old brother who was undernourished. In 1939, when the war broke out and Wysokie was burned down, Dina's family moved to Sokoly. Dina was 18 years old. She was slim, blonde, and friendly. She had the responsibility of providing food and wood for her family because her father had died. He was related to my grandmother, Alte Reva Wrobel (who was a

Krasnoborski before marriage). Dina often came to my Auntie Lea's house and Lea gave her food and clothing to wear.

Dina and I started out toward Wysokie in the evening, on foot. It was 16 kilometers one way. We walked all night. When we arrived, we bought 20 liters of oil and some meat. We spent the entire day at Auntie Pearl's house, and at nightfall, we each hung a parcel in front, on our chests, and one on our backs, and walked with these heavy loads, back to Sokoly. We had to keep moving, we couldn't rest because we had to walk under the cover of the night, being careful not to be caught. If the Germans found us, we would be shot. We used half of the oil and meat that I brought for the family and sold the other half. With the oil, we baked potato cakes. We had enough food for a short period of time, and when our food supply dwindled, we had to go to Wysoko again.

Laundry time was very difficult and trying for Lea and me. I had to go to the well and bring many buckets of water. The well was always crowded, with a queue, because only one bucket of water at a time could be fetched and people stood and gossiped while waiting for their turn.

The Sokoly hairdresser came to the well one morning when I was there. He was a joker. He told all the people waiting there, in a whisper: "I've got good news. The Germans lost the war. Do you hear the noise from the trucks on the highway? The Germans are retreating and this morning the first Russian envoy arrived in Sokoly." We all listened to him in silence. We believed him because we all clung to the hope that the war would end, and we would survive the nightmare. Then the hairdresser started to laugh. He told us that the Russian envoy was really a baby boy, born that morning to a woman named Goldka, fathered by a Russian officer who lived in her house. Everyone laughed with him, but it was laughter of hopelessness and despair.

NEWS OF NAZI ATROCITIES NEARBY

One morning in August 1941, 20 survivors from the neighboring town of Tykocin arrived in Sokoly. They told us about the massacre of the Jews of Tykocin. On the evening of August 24, the Germans had ordered all the Jews in Tykocin to assemble in the marketplace the next morning. They ordered them all to dress in their best clothing and to take all their necessities in one parcel, because they were going to be moved to the Bialystok ghetto. The next morning, they were divided into groups assisted by local police in the market square. However, they were not taken to Bialystok. Instead, they were marched to three pits in the Lupuchowo Forest. The pits had been prepared in the previous week on order of the German gendarmes using local villagers for labor. They were thrown into the prearranged pits and shot by machine guns.

Two of the survivors from Tykocin, two brothers aged 13 and 16, stayed with my Auntie Sorche. I talked to them, and they told me that because their parents were poor and didn't have nice clothing for them, they sent them to hide in the Lupuchowo Forest. Looking out from their hiding place in the thick bushes, they saw a big pit. They were eyewitnesses to the massacre. Group after group of naked people were being shot and thrown into the big hole, until the entire Jewish population of the town, about 5,000 men, women, and children, were murdered. That night, when everything was quiet, the boys left their hiding place and ran until they arrived in Sokoly.

A few months after hearing about this terrible incident, a group of Jewish workers from Sokoly were working at the railway station in Kruczewo. They were cutting stones and loading them on freight cars when a locomotive stopped near them. The driver of the train looked out of his window and told them: "If you knew what the Germans are doing to your people in Treblinka, you would not stay here and work so calmly. I am just coming from there, where a train full of Jews from the Warsaw ghetto was sent to the gas chambers to be gassed and burned. One trainload after another went there, and all the trains came back empty."

The workers heard what the train driver said. They came back to Sokoly and told the *Judenrat* [Jewish council). Everyone was broken-hearted. Nobody knew what to do. They were hard-working, peaceful people and could not even grasp the true horror of the situation. There were babies and elderly people, disabled and sick people. How could they abandon their loved ones? And where would they go?

WE FLEE TO THE FOREST

November 1, 1942, was a cold, but sunny, Sunday morning. Every Sunday, all the Poles from the surrounding villages and farms came to church in Sokoly and went back to their homes after the service. A few hours after the church service had ended, we saw a lot of the farmers running back to Sokoly. They came to collect unfinished orders from the Jewish tradesmen. Some went to the tailors to get materials or unfinished suits; others went to the shoemakers to take their unfinished boots or shoes.

The Poles told us the reason for their panic: the Germans were travelling around the countryside from village to village, ordering all the farmers to bring their horses and wagons to Sokoly the next morning. They had ordered 600 empty wagons for early Monday morning. They told them that the vehicles were needed to collect wood from the forest, but the farmers understood that the real reason for bringing the wagons was to evacuate all Jews from Sokoly and send them to the gas chambers in Treblinka, the same as had been done in other towns in the vicinity.

Chaim Yehoshua Olsha, a respected member of the Judenrat, confirmed that 600 horses and wagons had been ordered for Monday morning. He advised the people to do as they thought fit.

The people knew what to expect. They understood that this time, it was Sokoly's turn. The Jews were running around, asking each other, "What shall we do? How can we run away and leave our houses, our warm beds? What about the old, the sick, and the little children?"

I listened to these questions, but my mind was already made up: I would never give in to those crazy killers who were playing God, deciding who should live and who should die. I knew that I had the same right to live in this world as they did. If they, the German bosses had been normal, they would have understood that the world is made for all people alike, especially for those with a pure heart and clean hands, which is what I considered myself to be. They would understand that we are all here only for a limited time and that they, the crazy Nazis, had no right whatsoever to kill anyone. They were only mortals. who would themselves die in due course. My only question was: "With whom shall I run away?"

My cousin Dina Krasnoborski asked me to come with her. She told me that a group of girls who worked with her digging turf in the Bruszewo Forest for the Germans, were going to the forest to hide. They knew the countryside well and would try to save themselves. I asked Auntie Lea what she was going to do. She said that her family was also going to run away. I decided that I would go with Lea, Manes (Tabak) and their four children.

Lea locked up the cupboards and doors and made sure she had all of the keys. We then took the twins, taking turns carrying them. They were 11 months old, very beautiful babies. The two older children, Leibele, aged seven, and Faigele Cipora, five, held on to their mother's skirt.

We headed toward my other aunt's home. Sorche (Goldberg), her husband Pesach Tabak, and their five children were also ready to leave. Grandmother Hinka Tabak told us to go. She told her son Pesach not to worry; she would stay and look after the house, and nobody would steal his hard-earned possessions. This was my grandmother who had come back to Poland from America.

Hinka was the most generous, good-hearted, unselfish woman I knew. She was always working, always helping the whole family as much as she could. Now, she was powerless. She just looked at her children with her large, deep-set eyes, eyes of despair and tragedy, and urged us to go, to try to save ourselves.

Sokoly is surrounded by forests on all sides and all the people who fled the town headed there. There were villages near the forests where the Jews had Polish friends, whom they trusted and with whom they had dealt all their lives. My uncles and their families decided to try to reach the forest close to the village of Sklody-Borowe, near their parents' farm.

We left Sokoly in the late afternoon, almost evening, of Sunday, November 1, 1942. Nobody stopped us until we reached the Kruczewo Forest. It was autumn and the night was freezing cold. We were dressed warmly, with two layers of clothing, but after we sat on the ground for a few hours, we began to shiver from the cold.

In the forest we met my auntie Leah's youngest sister, Toiba, her husband Alter Digholtz, and their beautiful, blonde two-year-old daughter, Shifra. Toiba was very beautiful. She was the most beautiful woman in Sokoly. Shifra complained a lot. "Why are we sitting here in the forest on the ground and in the cold? Why am I not in my bed?" she asked. Toiba stood up and said, "She is right. If we are going to die anyway, I want to die in my own bed." She and her small family left the forest and went home, back to Sokoly.

In the morning, Uncle Manes said that he thought he should go to work in Lapy, as usual, even from the forest. He thought that it might be a false alarm and if it were, they would be killed for not going to work. Most of the other workers from Sokoly, who were also in the forest, left with their rucksacks and headed toward the train station. Suddenly we heard shooting. The men who had just left the forest met a group of SS men with rifles, ready to shoot. A few of the men were shot, the rest ran back into the forest.

We headed toward the village of Sklody, where the entire Tabak family had lived and worked for many years after they came back from America. Uncle Pesach had good Polish non-Jewish friends there, he thought that they would help him and his family. He planned to find jobs for his three daughters as servants, and he was full of confidence.

We walked only at night. In the daytime, we had to hide in the forest. No one in the villages we passed would let us into their homes, not because they were so cruel, but because they were frightened that their neighbors would inform on them.

The Germans had ordered the Poles not to give food or shelter to a Jew, on the penalty of death. There were informers in each village, "secret police" who were paid by the Germans.

It started snowing and it was very cold. The young twins cried constantly because they were cold and hungry; nothing we did would stop them from crying. Lea (Goldberg) Tabak received milk from a farmer in exchange for some stockings. We tried to give the cold milk to the babies, but they refused to drink it.

It had already been five long days and nights and in all this time the twins did not have anything to eat or drink. They were living on a small amount of sugar that their mother put in their mouths every day. We all knew they would not last long under those conditions, and so it was decided to do something drastic in order to save their lives.

We heard a horse and wagon approaching on the road. Lea and Manes laid the screaming twins at the side of the road, and we all hid in the bushes and watched. The farmer stopped, picked up the screaming babies, put them in the back of his wagon and drove into the village. After that, Lea banged her head on the trees and cried all day long.

We walked every night through forests and fields until we reached Sklody. There, we waited near a barn while Pesach and Manes went inside their friend's house. After a long time, they came out with the Polish non-Jewish friend, who brought us a pot of hot soup and some bread. He explained to us that we could not stay in his house because he was frightened that he would be punished by death if caught by the Germans.

There were Polish informers in the village who would tell the Germans about us. They would kill his family for harboring Jews. The Polish friend promised that if we came after dark and made sure that nobody saw us, he would always give us food and a place to sleep in his barn. We thanked him and walked back to the forest.

It started to snow heavily. It was very cold. In the darkness, we saw an isolated farmhouse and went inside. The farmer talked to my uncles; he said that we had no chance of survival, unless we could make it to the bigger forests, where we might be able to meet and join a group of Russian partisans. He said that was our only chance. I heard them talking and I thought to myself, *If only God will help me find and join a partisan group, I will have a chance to live.*

The farmer gave us some food and permission to sleep overnight in his barn. Pesach told him that I knew how to sew, and he let me stay there, but the others had to leave. I sewed for the farmer's family for three days. On the third evening, I had to go. A German Major came to tell the farmer that, in the morning, the Germans were coming to collect wheat. I had to walk to the forest alone for the first time. I was very lonely and sad, and my heart was heavy.

I came to a small house surrounded by trees and knocked on the door. In that house lived a farmer, his wife and their two children. They were poor but kind people. Due to the long distance, I had walked, my shoes were ruined. The man asked me if I had money to buy new shoes. I told him I did not. He looked at my shoes and said that if I continued to walk in those broken shoes without any soles, my feet would freeze. He said he would help me; he cut soles from wood and nailed them to my old leather shoes. I now had good shoes. The farmer let me stay in his house. I helped his wife with housework and did some sewing for the children.

One day, when I was sitting and eating at the table in the farmer's home, a neighbor showed up unexpectedly and saw me there. The farmer became very nervous after that; he told me that I had to leave his house that evening. The visiting neighbor was a member of the AK, the *Armia Krajowa* [Home Army], a Polish underground organization that fought against the Germans, but also killed Jews and Russians.

I left as soon as it became dark. I tried to walk to another farm, but darkness covered the world. I couldn't see a thing; I was like a blind person. I walked in pitch darkness through meadows and fields, without having any idea where I was going. It didn't matter anyway. I felt such injustice! I was only 17; I had not even seen or tasted life's wonders.

Sometimes I lost hope, but I had such a strong will to live that I just kept on going. Every fiber in my body kept hoping for another day, another hour. The more dangerous it became, the more they wanted to rob me of my life, the more precious and important my life became to me. The only things that kept me going were my will to live and my wish to see God's beautiful world.

I walked all night long. I must have been 16 or more kilometers away from the farm I had left. The sky began to turn gray. I stopped and listened. I could hear a dog barking and I followed the sound. From a distance, I could see a man working in his field and decided to ask him the name of the place.

As I moved closer, the surroundings became more visible. I could see that everything looked familiar. I thought, *Oh well, a lot of farms look the same*. I looked again. It was the same man whom I had left the previous evening! When I reached the farmer, he asked me why I had returned. I was shocked, surprised and astonished to think that I had walked all night in circles, when I meant only to go forward. I didn't know how to explain; I just apologized and walked away. When they taught me in school that the earth is round, I didn't believe it. But then, I decided that it is true; the earth is round and round.

Soon, day broke, and I saw another isolated farmhouse as I walked across a field. I went inside, where a pale woman was working at a spinning wheel and a young girl was sitting at a table in a corner, plucking feathers from a chicken. The girl was so absorbed in her work that she didn't even turn to look at me. I looked again at her familiar face. It was true; I was not mistaken! It was Uncle Pesach's youngest daughter – 13-year-old, freckle-faced, Perale.

Perale told me that her father had met Sasinowski, the farmer, chopping wood in the forest and he agreed to take her home with him, to help his ailing wife with various jobs. Perale looked like she was Polish, but she spoke Polish with a heavy accent, so the farmer told her to pretend that she was deaf and dumb. People visited this isolated farm very seldom, and it looked like a safe place to hide.

Perale said that maybe I would also be allowed to stay for a few days; it all depended on the farmer's mood. Sasinowski was moody; one minute he was kind, and the next, he would lash out and beat his wife and two sons. The farmer's wife was kind and friendly, but she had no say in any decisions. Sasinowski was to return in the evening from the market. Only then would he decide whether or not I would be allowed to stay. In the meantime, the woman gave me some housework and sewing to do. She was very happy that I knew how to work on her sewing machine.

Sasinowski arrived home in a good mood. He didn't even ask what I was doing there. He just kept talking about the Jews and how stupid they were. He had seen a young shepherd boy taking a group of barefoot, half-frozen Jews to the Germans to be killed, and they didn't even resist. The farmer showed hatred toward Jews, but he did not tell me to leave. Instead, he prepared a place for Perale and me to sleep. In the morning, he told me that I could stay and do sewing for his wife. I felt very happy, but my happiness lasted only a short time.

One morning, Sasinowski told us that the *Soltys* [the mayor or leading official of a Polish town or village] had notified all the farmers in the vicinity that the next day, the German

Amtskommissar was coming to register and stamp the best pigs, and Perale and I would have to go to the forest to hide for the day.

The next morning, all the farmers took their best pigs to the forest to hide them. Sasinowski also ordered his older son to do the same. I thought that we should follow and hide together with the pig, but I saw that the boy didn't want us to come with him. Perale and I went to the closest part of the forest and sat all day under a tree. We were hungry and cold and impatient, waiting for the day to end, so we could go back to the warm house and have some food.

That night, when we arrived back at the farm, we found Sasinowski's wife crying. She told us what had happened. Instead of taking the pig to hide in the forest as his father had ordered, her son took it down the main road. Precisely at that time, the German Amtskommissar was conducting a raid on that road. He stopped the boy, stamped the pig, and ordered the boy to take the pig to the Szepietowo railway station.

When Sasinowski discovered what had happened, he was furious. He beat his son and his wife and blamed the Jews for everything before leaving the house. The farmer's wife warned us to run away before Sasinowski returned; she did not know what he would do to us in his fury. We were so tired, disappointed, and upset that we did not want to run away. We just sat on the floor and mourned both the pig and our bad luck. When Sasinowski returned, he shouted and yelled at his wife and to himself, but he ignored us. He did not even look at us. We sat there on the floor all night and left the farm at dawn.

We arrived at a big farm near Sklody, the village where my mother was born and raised. We went into the farmhouse and recited a Christian morning blessing, the way all Polish Christians did. The farmer's family thought that we were Polish girls hiding so that we would not be deported to Germany to work in forced labor. I spoke perfect Polish, but I could not lie. I told them that we were Jewish girls and that we were from Pesach Goldberg's family. They all knew Pesach, the blacksmith.

The woman of the house told us that we could be saved if we pretended to be Polish. I knew that in daylight people could tell that I was Jewish, due to my dark facial features: dark eyes and black hair. Also, I was not good at pretending to be non-Jewish. Perale looked Polish, but she spoke Polish with an accent, but the woman insisted that she would help us and that we must try to pretend. She said she knew that the wife of the Soltys in Sklody had four small children and was pregnant again. She had to make big parties for the Germans when they arrived each Sunday and was in desperate need of help.

The good woman took me to the house of the Soltys. She vouched for me, saying that she knew my family. She advised me to say that I was born in Novogrudok, that my parents had been taken to work in Germany and that I wished to work as a housemaid. The wife of the Soltys was very happy and asked me how much money I would like for a year's wages. I answered that first she had better see my work, and then we could decide about money.

I started working, peeling potatoes, sweeping the floors, looking after the children, sewing on the machine, but when I went to the shed to get firewood, the neighbors looked at me with suspicion. They came to the house and whispered to Soltys's wife. Then they asked me what parish my family belonged to and wondered why they didn't see me in church. I began to think that I should leave and that I would be safer away from the neighbors who suspected that I was Jewish.

One evening, we heard shooting and screaming. The family of the Soltys went into hiding. The wife told me that Russian partisans had come to one of the local farms to get food. When the farmer refused to open the door, the partisans set fire to the farm. I went outside and saw that the whole village was burning. I could hear cries from the animals and yells from the farmers who were riding on horses and trying to save their homes and animals. There was shooting and shouting. I didn't return to the house. Instead, I went to the house where Perale was staying to fetch her, and we left the village together.

Perale told me that after my uncle's family had left me at the farm, her two older sisters, Feigel and Toiba, had also been separated from the rest of the family. One evening, the whole family went to sleep in an empty barn in the middle of the Lopienie Forest. Suddenly, in the middle of the night, they were awakened by two men with torches, pointing guns at them. They didn't know if the men were from the Polish AK or the German secret police. In either case, they thought it was the end of their lives.

It turned out that the two men were actually Russian partisans. They asked the parents if the two older girls could join them. They promised to look after them and protect them. The parents knew that the girls would have a better chance of survival with the partisans, so they agreed. Sixteen-year-old Feigel and 15-year-old Toiba left with the men.

Now, Perale and I thought that we should try to find her sisters and the partisans and join them, and then hopefully we would also have a better chance to survive. These girls, Feigel and Toibe, knew where Perale was staying. We thought that maybe they would look for her there, so we went back to Sasinowski's house and asked if any member of our family had come looking for us. The woman replied that Feigel had come to the house looking for us after we left. She was dressed well, the woman said, and looked beautiful. She had a pair of shiny boots and a red scarf with flowers. She left a message that we should look for her in the village of Jeczkas.

We were very happy to receive Feigel's message. We left Sasinowski's farm, and kept asking for directions, until we found Jeczkas. It was still dark, before daybreak, when we arrived. We knocked on people's doors, recited the morning blessing and asked if anyone had seen a girl with a red scarf. Many of the people had seen Feigel passing through the village, but they did not know where she had gone.

Finally, a man told us confidentially that on the other side of that village there was a small forest. In that forest was a house that belonged to a man named Pasink. He would be able to tell us where the girls and the Russian partisans were located. When we arrived near the house in the forest, we were greeted by a very big dog that barked at us, but the owner came out, controlled the dog, and invited us to come inside.

How surprised and pleased we were, when we came into the house, to see Feigel and Toiba. They told us what had happened to them since they separated from the family. They had wandered through fields and forests with the two Russian men; Toiba with Wanka Smyrnov, who was about 35 years old, and Feigel with the other man, until they came to a forest near Bransk, where they met a whole group of Russian partisans.

Three Jewish girls from Bransk were with the partisans: Stella (Lerner), Adella, and another girl. The partisans would take the girls from farm to farm, ordering the farmers to look after them for one week. They warned each farmer that if something bad happened to the girls, they would shoot his family and burn his farm. The farmers obeyed the partisans; they each kept the girls for a week and treated them well.

One morning, Germans surrounded the partisan group and began shooting. The members of the group ran in panic in different directions, and Feigel and Toiba found themselves separated from the others. Toiba and Feigel came to Pasink's house. They told him that the Russians had ordered them to stay in his house for three days. Since this was already the third day, they had to leave that night. The only thing to do now was to try to find either the partisans, or their own family.

Much later, I met Stella, and she told me her story. Stella was a student. She was 18 years old, tall, and pretty, with black shiny hair and a fair complexion. Her mother and father were both dentists. Stella's father had at one time been an officer in the Polish army. Both of Stella's parents were tall and intelligent and spoke only

Polish. Her mother entertained a lot and used to invite the intelligentsia in Bransk to her home for dinner. Even in the ghetto, the German police were frequent guests at dinners in their house.

When the Germans surrounded the Bransk ghetto, Stella and her friend Adella ran away to the forest. Stella was hungry and afraid of being killed. Her whole body was alert and full of fear. Every sound, even the snapping of a twig, caused her fear and anguish. In the forest, the girls met some Russian men on the run who called themselves partisans. They were wild, lonely, hunted men and the girls married them, hoping they would be protected. Stella married Pietka, a blond, friendly, good-hearted young man who tried to protect her from hunger and danger. She felt safe and happy with him.

A few Jewish boys were also hiding in that forest. Pietka befriended one of them and asked him to take care of Stella if something should happen to him. Stella thought that it was absurd for him to talk like that. Pietka was her hero, her strong protector. He had a gun, and nothing could happen to him. One day, some of the partisans went out and Pietka and two others didn't return. They had been killed.

Stella was devastated. She was pregnant and alone. The young Jewish boy whom Pietka had befriended looked after her and brought her food. When she was due to have her baby, he took her to a bunker in the forest, where a Jewish family was hiding. In that bunker, the family had dug a drainage hole to prevent flooding. Every night, they would fill up about ten buckets of water, which they spilled outside, at a distance from the bunker. When Stella arrived, the family took their possessions and moved out of the bunker.

Stella was left alone; the boy called an old woman from the forest to help with the birth, and a baby girl was born. The baby was blonde, like Pietka. The old lady and the boy left, and Stella was alone again. She was sure that she was going to die. Stella told me that when the old lady delivered the baby, she didn't feel any pain;

she felt nothing, as if she were dead, as if some other woman was having a baby and she was just an onlooker, an outsider, a ghost, or a spirit.

Slowly, the bunker became flooded. It was full of water and Stella moved the baby and herself to the edge, where it was a bit drier. She waited for the Russians, Pietka's good friends, to come and take the baby to a home, or perhaps to some farmer. It was snowing. The owner of the bunker hired a half mad, crazy Jew from the forest and sent him to take the baby away to be buried. Stella refused. She sent the man to call for the Russians, to let them help her decide and tell her what to do.

The next day, Pietka's best friend, Paul Rasin, came with another man to see Stella. They told her that the whole forest was surrounded by Germans, and therefore, they could not move her somewhere else. They told her that she should let that crazy man take the baby away. There was no other solution. They said, "We are in a war. The owner and his family need this bunker free for their own use!" Stella did not further protest. It was useless; she could not do a thing. She was helpless and weak. The man came back, took the baby, and left. Stella could never forget what happened to her in that forest.

Later, Stella met her mother and father. They told her that they had been hiding in a bunker in the ghetto. The ghetto had already been emptied of Jews. When all their food was finished, they went outside and walked through the town. The Germans, who used to come to the family's dinners, saw them and did not stop them; they let them go. They had wandered from farm to farm, paying 50 dollars per night to sleep in each house. Now they were united with their daughter and all of them left together to meet their fate.

The four of us: Feigel, Toiba, Perale, and I, were determined to find either the partisans or our family. We asked a lot of people if they had seen the partisans, and they told us that they were asking around, looking for the girls, but the girls had left, and nobody knew where they had gone.

We walked for many nights, until we reached a familiar village named Zochy. We asked the people of the village where we could find Pesach's family. They told us that to find them, we should wait until dark and listen to hear in which house the dogs were barking the loudest; the family would be in that house. We listened to the barking of the dogs, and sure enough, there they were, in the house where the dogs barked the loudest, standing near the barn. It was a very happy reunion between the mother, the father, and their daughters.

We sat together in the forest around a fire and shared our experiences. We loved to be together, but I knew how dangerous it was to stay in a group and how very exposed and unprotected we were. I knew that it would be easier for the two of us to find food and shelter than it would be for our entire group of 12.

I decided to take one of the girls with me and leave. I wished to take beautiful, easy-going, talkative Feigel with me, but Toiba insisted that she wanted to come instead. Feigel gave in and said, "It's all right, let Toiba go." So, I took good-looking, serious, quiet, 16-year-old Toiba with me, and we left. We said goodbye to the family and went, with sad hearts, to meet our fate.

WANDERINGS

We walked from village to village, from house to house. Everywhere we went, the Poles gave us food, but they were too frightened to let us stay, or to give us work or shelter. At night, we had nowhere to sleep. It was snowing and windy. We walked until we came to a farm where we had previously stayed with my uncle, Pesach Tabak.

The owner of the farm was a widower. He was lazy and a bit crazy. He owned 25 acres, but he didn't work his land. He had three daughters. The oldest daughter, who was 17 years old, had the mentality of a six-year-old. Every day, she went to the pasture to look after the cow. The 12-year-old, Genka, was the boss of the family. The youngest daughter was six years old. The father walked around, visiting nearby farms and villages, taking his meals with the farmers, while his children were starving at home.

When an old man from a neighboring farm died, his family brought the widower's children the leftovers from the after-funeral party, and they had a feast. I had heard Genka praying that another neighbor would die soon, so that she and her sisters would have food to eat.

As we came to the house, Genka did not want to let us in, but when we showed her a piece of bread through the window, she opened the door. We gave Genka our bread and she let us sleep on the floor that night, but we had to leave in the morning.

We walked in daylight, through fields and forests until we arrived in an unfamiliar village. We opened the door of the first house at the end of the street and went inside. When the farmer saw us, he looked worried, but didn't say a word. Sitting at the table was a well-dressed stranger. He looked at us stood up, looked at his watch and said, "I have a lot of work to do today. I must take two more Jewish girls to Piekuty, to the nearest German police station."

I immediately understood the situation. We had walked into that house and met an informer, a German spy! We stood speechless. My heart was thumping hard, and I had no idea what to do. Suddenly, the man changed his mind; he took the farmer aside and whispered something in his ear. Then, aloud, he said, "Give these girls some food. I will give it a pass this time." We calmed down, the farmer gave us some food, we thanked him and left.

Toiba and I walked along the road that led through the forest. It was peaceful and quiet; not a soul was seen or heard. We were talking, without caution or any cause for alarm. Suddenly, we heard a noise, the pounding of a horse's hooves. We looked around and saw a man riding toward us on a galloping horse, shouting: "Girls, run into the forest. Save yourselves, the Germans are coming!"

We left the road and went into the forest. A few moments later, through the trees we saw a horse pulling a wagon loaded with Germans on the way to the village. We later learned that the informer had sent these Germans to kill us. I understood that, once again, I had received help from Heaven and a Guardian Angel was looking after me.

In the forest we didn't feel the cold as much as in the fields because the trees protected us from the wind. But we were always alert, always aware of danger. Each part of the forest belonged to a different farmer. There was always a commotion in the forest. The farmers would come to their portions of the forest to gather leaves, to cut wood, or to pasture their cattle. We tried to stay hidden in the thickest bushes. We made sure no one would see us, since it was safer. We kept close to the road because we were afraid of getting lost in the forest and not being able to find the road in the dark.

One Sunday evening, we arrived in the village of Hodiszewo. We were thinking of asking for food and maybe a place to sleep for the night. We opened the door of the first house and went inside. We saw a middle-aged couple and their daughter, who were entertaining a well-dressed, nice-looking young man. The young man was a German, dressed in civilian clothing. We saw how the girl's parents looked at us and then at each other in shock.

The man stood up and told us in German, "Show me your passports." I pretended to be Polish, and said that our passports were home and that we would go and bring them to him. We started towards the door, but the German followed us out of the house and shouted: "*Halt!*" We heard a shot and the girl's shrill voice, asking him to come back inside.

We kept on going, and then we ran, as fast as we could. It was dark and cold, and we were very hungry. We had to try our luck elsewhere. We walked in a different direction, until we came to another village. We arrived at a house where a young woman was engaged in conversation with an older man. After we said an evening blessing, we asked for some food and permission to stay overnight. The woman turned to the man for an answer. It turned out that the man was her father, and he was the Soltys of the village. His reply was: "*Owszem*," which means "with pleasure."

The Soltys left the house, and his daughter gave us some food and put out straw for us to sleep on. For the first time in a long time, we were very happy. That night, everything seemed to be all right. I forgot all my worries and problems and concentrated on that night only. We slept well. When we woke up in the morning, I told Toiba that we should leave early before anyone saw us. The housewife was very calm. She was not a bit worried. She told us to stay and have breakfast.

That afternoon, we walked to a neighbor's house, where a young widow lived with her two-year-old daughter and her old father. The woman asked me to make a little dress for her daughter from one of her old dresses. I turned the material to the other side, and it looked like new. I made a beautiful dress for the little girl. The mother was so happy that she took the finished dress and showed it to all the women in the village. She told me that everybody agreed that I was a good dressmaker.

A woman who lived in the neighborhood came to me and secretly asked me to come to her house whenever I had some free time, to sew vests for her and her daughters. She told me to be careful, to come only at night, and to make sure that no one would see me. I felt that this woman was clever and honest because she was cautious.

This village, Lendowo-Budy, became a legendary refuge for a lot of wandering Jews, who called it "the Garden of Eden." Everywhere else, no one would let Jews stay; here, the people opened their doors wide, without any fear. Soon there were Jews in every house in the village.

Two Jewish tailors from Bransk arrived in Lendowo with their sewing machine. They made suits for the village men from new material. They also made suits from old ones, by turning the fabric over on the other side. A girl from Warsaw knitted beautiful sweaters. A mother from Lapy and her two daughters were staying at other houses. The dentists, the Lerners from Bransk, paid American dollars for accommodation.

We came to a neighbor's house. Sorche, Toiba's mother, was there with her three-year-old son, sitting and making house slippers. Feigel and Perale were working in another house. Pesach and his 13-year-old son Moshe were hiding in another village, at the home of a rich farmer. The farmer wanted Pesach to survive, so he would have a good blacksmith for his large farm.

While I was still working at the widow's house, one of the neighbors, a man named Perkowski, came and asked me to come to his place to help with the housework. He had three young children and his wife had just given birth to another baby. The wife was weak and bedridden after the birth. He worked in another village as a hired hand because he didn't own any farmland.

I told Perkowski that he would have to ask the Soltys's permission for me to go with him, because I would have to go to the well to fetch water and would be seen during the day. The Soltys gave his permission, and I started working for Perkowski's family. I baked bread, cooked potatoes, and cabbage, washed the clothing and linens. I slept on top of the oven and would climb up and down the stairs at night to help the children.

Perkowski told me that he needed flour for a christening party. I had to work on a hand-mill. This was a grindstone that rubbed one stone onto another, grinding the grains of wheat to produce flour. I turned that grindstone every night until midnight. It was so difficult that I thought my arm would break. When the farmer asked me if it was too hard to do, I answered that it was all right; I would do it for as long as necessary.

One morning, Perkowski's wife told me to take a bucket and milk the cow. I had never in my life even stood close to a cow. I was afraid that the cow would kick me or even kill me, but I had to do it. Nobody ever showed me how to do the milking. I had to use my imagination.

When I thought I had finished milking, I brought the bucket with the milk into the house. The woman accused me of drinking a lot of the milk myself, because it was not the usual amount. I explained to her that I did not drink this milk, not even a drop, but I thought that I couldn't draw any more milk from the cow; I had never milked a cow in my life! The woman understood. She sent her nephew to finish the job.

Perkowski's 22-year-old nephew also lived in his house. He was part of a group of bandits who killed Jews, undressed them, and sold their clothing. If they found money hidden inside the clothes, they used it to buy vodka or *samogon* [homemade vodka], throw parties, and drink until they were very intoxicated. Then they would go and look for other Jews to kill.

I used to serve this bandit his dinner. He would talk about Jews and how he hated them. He said he could kill Jews without remorse. He also admitted that he liked me, said he felt that I was no different from him. He said he didn't mind my living there and that he wouldn't kill me, because I didn't have any valuables, not even a pair of good shoes, only wooden ones. I heard the farmer Perkowski telling his nephew that, one day, God's wrath would fall on him and his bandit friends for killing innocent people, and that they would be punished.

I enjoyed working and living at Perkowski's, but eventually, his wife got stronger. She was out of bed and able to resume her housework, and I had to leave. Toiba and I went to Leopoldowa's house. She was the lady who told us to come over at the night to sew vests for her and her daughters. When we approached the front gate, we were greeted by eight savage dogs. I thought they would kill us, but the owner came out; he controlled the dogs, and we were able to go inside. They gave us food and a place to sleep, and we were very grateful. We worked in a spare room, and nobody knew about us, so we felt safe.

One evening, we heard a commotion and noise. People were running around in the village. The husband went to inquire. He came back and told us that there had been a town meeting. All of the villagers had been advised to tell the Jews to go to the forest the next morning. As for Toiba and I, he agreed with his wife that we could stay in the house, because nobody knew we were there.

On that particular morning in January 1943, the forests around Lendowo-Budy were surrounded by Germans hunting for the Jews who were hiding there. These Jews were from the nearest towns: Bransk, Wysokie, Lapy, Ciechanowiec, and others. The Germans murdered many Jews that day. Polish farmers who were driving through the forest from the market watched the killings.

A farmer told our host that he had watched the murders of three of my closest relatives. He knew who they were because he was familiar with them. He saw the Germans killing these three innocents. He watched the execution of Toiba's older sister, the beautiful, vigorous, 17-year-old Feigel, who was full of life; of good-hearted, tall, slim Perale, who was just 14 years old; and beautiful, strong Uncle Manes Tabak, who was only 28 years old. Uncle Manes struggled with the Germans, but he was overpowered and shot. Feigel asked the German why he was doing this. The answer was a bullet. She ran away bleeding but was shot again from behind and died. Perale was also shot dead.

When we heard about the shootings, our hearts ached. People had often told us how many Jews had been killed in the forests, but when they told us of the killing of our own family, of people we loved, the impact was immense. Our own hopeless situation was made even more evident to us. We were surrounded by death and thought it was only a matter of days, or maybe even hours, before our turn came, unless God would protect us.

We left the village of Lendowo-Budy and came to a crossroad. There were three roads heading in different directions. We picked one of the roads, without knowing where it led. It was a frosty night. The ground was icy and frozen. We walked with care, because with each step the ice would break, making a loud noise. We saw a light coming from a house and walked toward it. A dog started barking and we heard someone firing shots from a short distance away. We quietly sat down on the ground and didn't move for many hours. Finally, we left the place. Later, we learned that a German Amtskommissar lived in that house.

The next evening, we wanted to cross a very long, but narrow river, to go to villages on the other side where we had never been before. We picked up a long stick to measure the depth of the river, and we tried to find a shallow place so we could cross the river on foot. We walked for hours, measuring the depth. Toiba began to cry from exhaustion. I tried to cheer her up. I joked, looked at the funny side, told her to think that we were engineers measuring rivers.

Eventually, we found a shallow place and crossed to the other side of the river. We stayed all day in the forest near the river. At sundown we crossed a field, and in the evening, we arrived in a village. We came to a house and found the door unlocked. We called, but nobody answered. No one was inside the house; it was empty and dark inside. We felt around in the darkness and discovered a wooden sofa. We were hungry, but we were so exhausted that when we lay down on the sofa, we immediately fell asleep.

When we woke up in the morning, we saw a young Polish couple standing in front of us. They asked what we were doing there. I told them that we were Jewish, that we would like to work, and that we could do sewing or housework. The young wife was a kind woman; she told her husband that we didn't steal or take anything while the house was empty, and that this indicated that we were honest girls. He agreed that we could stay. The wife gave us food to eat and sewing to do, in a room next to the kitchen.

One day, a neighbor called. She had heard Toiba coughing and asked who was in the room. The young woman panicked, and we were forced to leave her house. We went to another house in the village. The woman there was pleasant; she gave us food and we talked. I took the broom and swept the floor. I was glad that the woman was pleased.

When it was nearly evening, the housewife's 15-year-old son suddenly burst into the room, looking very antagonized, and shouting: "Girls, run into the yard and hide! Somebody informed the police, and they are on the way to the village; they are coming to kill you!" We ran into the yard to hide, but the yard was empty. There was nowhere to hide in the yard.

In the open field at the end of the yard, there were two very long buildings for storing grain. We noticed a long, very narrow space between these two barns. We pushed ourselves into that space sideways and sat on the ground, one behind the other. It was dark and cold. We had already been sitting there for a while when Toiba started to complain that her feet were frozen. The soles of her shoes were worn out. She was chilled and felt miserable. Toiba suggested that we go back to that nice woman's warm house. She thought that the police had already left because it was dark.

When we had already reached the yard of the house, Toiba was the first one to notice the policeman in the yard because his white armband stood out in the dark. She screamed out to alert me and she managed to run away, but the man caught my arm in an iron grip and didn't let me free myself. I was terrified. I tried desperately to think of something. I knew that my Polish was perfect and in the dark he would not be able to tell that I was Jewish.

I started to shout. "Look," I said, "you are holding me, a Polish girl, and you let the Jewish girl run away!" He let go of my arm and I ran back to the place where Toiba and I had been hiding before. I felt inside; Toiba was already sitting there. The policeman blew his whistle, and more police came running. We could hear and even see them all running past our hiding place, except for the last policeman. He stopped and investigated our hiding place. I saw him and felt like the Angel of Death was staring me in the face. My heart stopped beating from fear. I held my breath, so as not to make any sound.

Then to my amazement, and with miraculous relief, I heard the policeman call to the others: "They are not here either." He shone his flashlight above our heads. We were sitting on the ground, and he did not see us. The policeman left, running around, and searching for us with his companions. We could still hear noises, so we sat in the same spot for many hours, until midnight. Then we stood up, straightened our stiff limbs, and came out of our hiding place. We walked through the field into the forest, across the river, and back to the familiar village of Lendowo-Budy.

In the evening, we knocked at Perkowski's door. His wife let us into the house. She gave us an old, large coat to undo. She wanted us to turn over the fabric and sew up a smaller coat for her 11-year-old daughter. During the day we did the sewing in a little back room, hidden from any onlookers. At night, we slept in the cellar where the potatoes were kept.

On the fourth evening, Perkowski's wife came home from a town meeting. She told us that the Soltys had advised the villagers to tell the Jews to go and spend the next day in the forest. We looked through the window and saw Jews walking towards the forest, which was only a short distance from the house. Toiba and I put on our coats and were also ready to leave, when the woman stopped us. She said that because the coat was not finished and nobody knew we were staying there, we didn't have to leave.

The next morning, we were sewing as usual, when we heard shooting from the direction of the forest. We panicked. The shooting had to be connected to the Jews. We looked out the window and saw German soldiers coming out of the forest. We looked out again and saw a vehicle standing near the Soltys's house at the other end of the village and a few Germans leaning against it. Mrs. Perkowski came running into our room, very distressed, shouting at us to run away. She said the Germans were going from house to house, looking for men to bury the dead in the forest.

I analyzed our situation. My instinct told me that we would be killed as soon as we went out in the open. I said to the woman, "The sun is shining so bright on the snow, and the Germans are on both sides of the street. We will be exposed, and they will shoot us for sure." But she insisted that we must leave right away. So, we put on our coats and scarves and left the house, walking around the back of the house.

We took the road to the forest. Toiba wanted to run, but I grabbed her arm. I even pinched her, and I whispered in her ear not to run, only to take big steps. We heard the Germans calling, shouting at us to stop. I told Toiba not to turn her head, to pretend that we were deaf and couldn't hear them. Finally, we reached the forest, and only then did we run as fast as we could. That part of the forest was not very large. We had to search to find a place where the bushes were thick enough to cover us. Finally, we sat down on the ground and waited for night to come.

NARROW ESCAPES

As soon as it became dark, we walked up to Piekutowska's farm, where Uncle Manes's six-year-old daughter Faigele (Cipora) was hiding. In the morning, Piekutowska told us that the Germans had killed all the Jews who were hiding in the forest near Lendowo-Budy.

Among those who were killed were Uncle Manes's wife, my Auntie Lea, and her seven-year-old son, Leibele. The boy was very devoted to his mother; he never let her out of his sight. When the Germans started shooting, the Jews all began to run away. A bullet hit Lea, but Leibele was far away, hidden in the bushes. When he could not see his mother near him, he turned back to look for her. He found her body and started to shake her. Then the Germans shot him, too.

Also killed were Mr. and Mrs. Lerner, the dentists from Bransk, and their daughter Stella. The girl from Warsaw who knitted sweaters in the village was also killed. All of them were buried in the same grave.

Piekutowska later told us that when we were walking on the road to the forest, the Germans had asked the Soltys who we were. He told them that we were smugglers from Warsaw. Two German soldiers started to follow us to the forest. They walked past Piekutowska's house toward the forest. They even asked her what direction we took. When they reached the forest, they decided not to chase us anymore, and they turned around and walked back to the village.

We were broken-hearted by the news about the murders of our relatives and friends. Piekutowska, seeing our distress, told us that our only hope was to pray, to ask God to help us. We sat with this religious woman for many hours that night. She prayed and we repeated the *Our Father* and *Hail Mary* prayers after her and we sang religious songs together with her throughout the night.

Piekutowska was a widow of about 50 years old. She was very religious, and the village people respected her. She lived on an isolated farm with her 27-year-old son. She owned a field and pigs, chickens and cows, but she could not do much work because she was an invalid and walked only with the help of a cane. Her son was lazy. He kept bad company; he drank a lot and didn't do much farm work.

When Uncle Manes and Auntie Lea came to Piekutowska's house on a cold winter night, she gave permission for their six-year-old daughter, Faigele, to stay with her when the others left. Before Faigele came to Piekutowska's house, when she was wandering around from village to village with her parents, the people used to say that she looked like the holy angels drawn in the pictures on their walls. She was a very beautiful little girl, blonde, with blue eyes and long, black eyelashes. Now, Faigele's parents and brother had been killed, and she was very grateful and happy to have a place to stay.

In the beginning, Piekutowska hid Faigele when the dogs barked, because it was a sign that strangers were coming. As time went on, she didn't hide Faigele anymore. Piekutowska risked her life for that little girl. She began to care for Faigele and loved her like her own. Piekutowska's son complained, so she told him to sleep in the village. She said that if the Germans came to kill her little girl, then they would have to kill her as well.

Faigele was a big help to the woman; she worked like an adult. She fed the pigs and carried wood for the fire. She stood on the table and painted the walls. She did the laundry, and in summer, she looked after the cows. She played with the young Polish girls in the fields and when they told her that the Jews killed Jesus, she would answer that she was sure that he was not killed by the Jews of Sokoly. Piekutowska taught Faigele to pray and took her to church every Sunday.

Now, Piekutowska gave some bread to Toiba and me, and we left. We remembered that the dog at Skludowska's farm in Lendowo-Budy did not bark at us, and we could walk quietly without alerting the owners and hide in their barn. We went into the barn, climbed up the ladder, and hid on top of the hay under the roof. We felt happy and safe, and we fell asleep. We stayed there for three days.

Our piece of bread had long ago been eaten and we were very, very hungry. We discussed the fact that nobody knew we were hiding in that barn. We would be able to return there, after getting some food. We came to the house of a woman to ask for food. People from the village kept coming into the house whispering to each other, looking at us in wonder as if they saw someone from another planet. We felt bewildered; we didn't know what was going on.

Then they told us that, that very day, two secret police had brought Toiba's father, Pesach, to the village of Lendowo-Budy, with his 14-year-old son, Moshe. Their feet and hands were tied with ropes. The secret police ordered the villagers to take Pesach and his son to the Germans in Piekuty, where they were killed.

Dombrowski, an important man in the village, told us that people had already called the Soltys to come and arrest us, but we were lucky, because the Soltys was already in bed and didn't want to come. Dombrowski took us to his house. He gave us milk and half a loaf of bread and told us to get as far away from the village as possible. We thanked him and left.

Toiba and I walked in pitch darkness. The night was bitterly cold. Both of us were feeling depressed and lonely. We knew that death was all around us and that there was no escape. We sat down on a big stone in the middle of a field to decide what to do. I knew the danger and stupidity of returning to the village and to the barn, but I also knew that nobody in the other villages would let us in. We had nowhere else to hide. I could not think of the past, or of the future, only of our immediate needs. Nobody knew that we had been hiding in that barn, so we decided to go back and hide there.

We arrived at the barn, climbed up inside, and found an egg. Now we had everything: an egg, some bread, and a place to sleep. In the morning, Andrei, the Russian worker, climbed up the ladder to collect eggs. Because he could not find any eggs in the usual place, he started looking further and found us. He called out to the woman who was milking the cows. She came up the ladder and told us to leave.

We were terrified. We knew that as soon as we were out in the open, we would be killed. When we came out of the barn, I took off my wooden shoes and looked around. I saw a lot of people gathering in the street. Toiba and I both started to run. We heard somebody chasing us. I was running barefoot, as fast as I could, and I was out of breath.

When I finally reached the woods I fell underneath a tree, but Toiba kept running. A big man, with a heavy piece of wood in his hand, caught me. Another man ran after Toiba. I asked the big, young bully if he was going to kill me, and he replied that he wanted to kill me. I told him to wait, and I would go and get Toiba, and we would come back together. He didn't answer, but he was thinking, considering my proposition.

I moved away and ran while he was standing there. Running through the forest, I noticed a deep hole. I jumped in and lay there for a few hours. When it was dark, I climbed out and started walking towards the farm where the widower lived with his three daughters. I was sure that the two men had caught Toiba. I asked the farmer to find out the next morning if a Jewish girl had been killed by the Germans in Piekuty. I thought that Toiba was dead, and that I was truly alone now. The farmer gave me permission to stay overnight. Somebody woke me up in the middle of the night. I opened my eyes and couldn't believe what I saw: It was Toiba, healthy and alive!

I was so happy and felt as if I had been given a new lease on life. Toiba told me what had happened to her. The two men did catch her. They took her to the Soltys in Lendowo-Budy. It turned out that when we ran away, through the village, the women of the village cried for our sake. The sister-in law of the Soltys begged him to let us go. When the men brought Toiba in, the Soltys took out some papers from his pocket and told them that she had documents, that she was Polish. Dombrowski gave the two men *kopniaks*, pants attached at the bottom to boots, and shouted at them. At the house of the Soltys, Toiba was given some food, and then she was set free. I thanked God that we had survived this ordeal and that we were still alive. I started to believe and hope that perhaps, with God's help, we would survive.

Early the next morning, we went to the farm that belonged to the farmer who had made my wooden shoes. I knew that he was a good, honest man, but it was no use going to his house. He would not let us in, because he was afraid, not only of the Germans, but also of his neighbors.

We found a hole in the ground where potatoes were kept. It was empty, so we jumped inside. We were happy and safe. I felt safest because nobody, not even the farmer, knew that we were hiding there. I knew that we were not at risk on this farm. If the owner found us, he would not kill us; he would only ask us to leave. We were sitting in the hole, relaxed, and talking in whispers.

Suddenly, we heard voices. We carefully looked outside and saw feet wearing boots – German soldiers' feet. The soldiers were carrying rifles on their shoulders. The farmer was working near the barn, close to our hole. We heard the soldiers asking him if he had seen any Jewish girls or bandits. The farmer was very calm and sure of himself. He told the Germans that they could look wherever they liked, but they would find no Jews or bandits on his property.

We were terrified. As soon as the soldiers' feet moved away, we covered ourselves with straw. We stayed in that hole until late at night. Then we went to the house and knocked on the door. When the farmer opened the door, he looked at me with an amazed look on his face. He couldn't figure out how I was still alive. He asked me, "Luba, tell me, how come so many Jews who passed my house were all killed? They were clever; some of them were blond; some had a trade. They had money, but nothing helped them. You are still alive. Who is helping you?"

I strained my mind, trying to find the answer to the farmer's question. It came to me that there was no other explanation, other than that God had sent an invisible helper to look after me. I gave my "helper" a hard time; I never understood that when I walked through fields in my wooden shoes, I made deep footprints. Whoever was in the business of catching Jews could always follow me. Only God's invisible helper, a guardian angel, protected me hundreds of times and that was why I was not killed. I answered the good man that I knew that God was helping me. He agreed. Then he said, "I should help you also."

The farmer warmed up some soup for us. We ate the hot soup, thanked him, and left in the night to find a hiding place, another shelter, for a day or two. We walked back to Lendowo-Budy and climbed up into Perkowski's barn. We fell asleep and I dreamed that I saw my dead mother and talked to her. I said to Mother, "They are chasing me. They wish to kill me. What shall I do?" In a very calm voice, my mother answered, "Don't be frightened, but now you have to climb up higher, higher." I woke up and immediately knew that I had to obey my mother.

Toiba could not understand why I was looking for a place to hide higher up in the barn. She asked, "What's wrong with this place?" I could not explain, but I knew that I had to find a higher place to hide. I looked again. There was another higher loft, filled with straw. I climbed up. Toiba reluctantly followed and I felt much better.

Not much later, we were looking down through the straw to the openings in the floor. We saw two bandits taking two guns out of a hiding place, where we had been sleeping before. If we had stayed there, they would have killed us. I understood that it was true; God was indeed helping me.

As soon as it got dark, we climbed down from the barn and walked to Piekutowska's house, where Faigele was hiding. Piekutowska introduced us to her cousin, an older man from the village of Pularie. The cousin had a proposition for Toiba. He wanted to take her to Pularie to work for him. Toiba was a very good slipper maker, and he wanted her to make a lot of slippers so he could sell them. He said that nobody would know that she was Jewish because she looked Polish. Toiba agreed and she left with the old man.

Piekutowska gave me supper. I thanked her and left the house. Outside, it was raining, and I looked for shelter. I saw the dog's kennel and called the dog's name. He knew me and did not even bark, but moved out and let me in. I slept there all night. In the morning, I looked out of the kennel and saw a hired helper working near the barn. I was afraid because I knew that he was not friendly. Then I saw Faigele going to the barn. She stopped and looked into the kennel and saw me. I was worried; I wasn't sure how she would react. I knew that my little cousin had mixed feelings about Jews; she was already brainwashed.

I heard the worker ask Faigele why she looked inside the kennel. "Did you think that your mother was hiding there?" I heard her answer, "There's nobody inside that kennel. I know that my mother is dead. It's just an old habit." I was relieved. I stayed in the kennel all day, until nightfall.

In the forest near Lendowo-Budy, I met my Auntie Sorche (Goldberg) with her three-year-old son, Hershele. Sorche told me that she had made a deal with Janka Polonski from Lendowo-Budy. Sorche gave Janka an imitation fur coat, and in exchange, Janka agreed to hide her and the boy for a month. The coat was like new. In Poland at that time, it was very valuable.

Sorche suggested that I stay with her for one day in Janka's barn. She said Janka would not mind. I was glad to be with Sorche, even for a day. We sat in the barn on the straw and talked. At lunchtime Janka brought us a dish of thick noodles. I thanked her. I was grateful for the food, the company, and the place to hide for the day. Suddenly, on impulse, I turned around and looked out at the yard through an opening in the barn. I saw the tall, burly, young laborer who worked at Janka's house move towards the barn. In his hand, he held a long, sharp knife that was used for killing pigs. I understood that he had been hired by Janka to kill us.

I shouted to Sorche to move, to escape. We saw an opening from the barn to the cowshed. I crawled under the cows and then into the yard. I saw Sorche walking to Janka's house, and I followed her. We came inside where we met Janka's old father. Sorche told him that Janka had sent that laborer to kill us. She said that Janka had promised to keep her for a month, and today was only the first day of that month. Now, she wanted her coat back.

The old man called to Janka, who was upstairs, to bring down the coat. Janka came down and confirmed that she had sent the boy to kill us. But she refused to give the coat back to Sorche. Sorche cried, the old man shouted at Janka. Then Janka reluctantly gave Sorche the coat and we left the house. Sorche took her three-year-old son and her coat and walked away towards Sklody, where she hoped to find somebody who would let her stay for a while in return for her coat. I was alone again.

Janka was 28 years old. She was a bit plumpish, but she was blonde and pretty. When girls from the village were chosen to go to Germany for forced labor, they paid Janka and she would go in their place, but in a week or two, she would come back home. She told Perkowski that she slept with the German guards. They paid her a few times, and then they allowed her to leave and return home.

When I worked in Lendowo-Budy, the people would talk about Janka. They said that she was the village whore, that she was greedy, and that she would do anything for money. For many years, Janka had a boyfriend named Vicek Dombrowski. Janka told everybody that one day she would marry him. Although he came from a very respected family in the village, he later took on the role of the leader of a group of bandits who robbed and killed Jews hiding from the Germans. Janka's father, old man Polonski, was a well-respected farmer. Janka's older brother had a wife and children, and he was also held in high esteem. Janka, too, came from one of the nicest families in the village.

Vicek's younger brother, Stasiec, was honest and hard-working, but Vicek was just the opposite: lazy and a bandit. When there were no more Jews left in the area, he organized his gang of bandits to rob Polish farmers who were riding back with money from the markets. They pretended to be Russian partisans and robbed the farmers at gunpoint. The farmers recognized Vicek and told the priest his identity.

Although Vicek was a bandit and slept with Janka, he wanted very much to marry a nice, quiet girl from Polazie. The girl refused to marry him. Instead, she married an honest man from Sklody but Vicek never gave up. One night, he went to the man's farm and hung him in the barn. Then he married the widow.

One evening, Vicek's younger brother, Stasiec Dombrowski, came to Piekutowska's place, where Faigele was staying. He was very distressed. He told Piekutowska something he had seen. He had been riding back from the market in the dark, when he noticed that a light was shining from the grave where some Jews had been buried the week before. He stopped and quietly walked up to the place in the dark.

When he got there, he saw his brother Vicek with Janka, who was holding a lantern. They had dug out the dead and were pulling out their teeth because there were gold fillings in them. Stasiec Dombrowski was devastated to see how low his own brother had fallen. He didn't want to upset his parents by telling them about his brother's deplorable behavior and greed. He came instead to Piekutowska, who was religious and highly respected, to tell her what weighed heavily on his mind.

I felt that it was extremely unlikely that I would ever see Toiba again. I was hungry and cold and, worst of all, I was very lonely. I sat by myself in the bushes, under a tree. I felt the unfairness, the injustice that had been inflicted upon me, and I prayed to God. I prayed not from a book, but from inside my frightened, troubled, and broken heart.

When I walked alone, through forests, fields, and strange villages, during the freezing, cold winter nights, exposed to storms, winds, snow, rain and hunger, there were some kind people who helped me. Some good people gave me food and shared their warmth. They told me that they believed that God had sent a Messiah, born in Israel from a Jewish mother, who received a special power from God to help people in their greatest need. His name in Hebrew was Joshua, which means "help." They said that if I will believe with all my heart, then God would send him to help me survive, to live and to see God's beautiful, free world.

It was spring 1943, an exceptionally bright and sunny day. I walked through fields. From a distance, I heard the laughter and singing of free people who were working in the fields. I felt even more forlorn and forsaken, but with a desperate will to go on, to live. At nightfall, I arrived at a farm where I had stayed earlier during the winter with my uncles' families. The dogs barked at me, but the farmer came out and quieted them down and let me into the house. The farmer and his wife had two daughters and a cousin who was living with them. The cousin was a secret policeman for the Germans. The two girls were happy to see me because on previous visits I had told them beautiful stories and sang the latest Polish love songs to them. We went into a room and talked. I was waiting for the mother to call us for supper.

I looked around; the cousin had disappeared. When I asked where he had gone, the girls only looked at each other. I didn't feel comfortable. My instinct told me that I should leave, but I thought, *Maybe it's nothing to worry about. I should stay longer and wait for some food.* Then, suddenly, the younger girl said to me, "Luba, come outside with me." I went outside with her and stood next to the house. Although it was dark, I could see shadows coming towards the house on bicycles and could hear their approach. The young girl whispered to me, "Luba, run! Our cousin is coming with the Germans to kill you!"

I ran from the other side of the back yard towards the fields. I ran as fast as I could, and the darkness soon covered me. I ran through the field until I came to a small forest near Lendowo-Budy where I found a place to hide. After a time, I decided to walk towards the house of Leopoldowa, the good-hearted, clever lady for whom I had sewed the vests. I knew that the family had eight wolf-like dogs that would attack me, but I had to take the risk.

When I came to the gate, it was the middle of the night. I was very surprised to find that it was very quiet. No dog barked, there were no dogs to attack me. I didn't even bother to think why the dogs were not there, I just felt relieved. I walked straight up to the front door and knocked. I heard voices from inside, from behind the door, but nobody opened the door, so I waited and then knocked again. Then I heard a loud, nervous voice, saying: "Who is it?"

When I said it was me, the door opened and there was the son of the house, with an axe in his hand. When they saw that I was alone, they were no longer afraid, and he put the axe aside. They told me that when they heard knocking on the door, but didn't hear the dogs barking, they were sure that bandits had killed the dogs and stolen everything from the barn. They were afraid of such things happening because they were the richest family in a mostly poor village. The son was ready to kill whoever was at the door if the voice was not familiar.

They were glad that nothing was stolen and asked me to stay and do some sewing for them. The good woman took me to the top of the barn and gave me warm blankets to cover myself. In the morning, she woke me up and gave me hot food. I was so relieved, even though I knew it was only a temporary situation. For the time being, I felt like I was in the Garden of Eden.

In this barn, in warmth and peace, after such a long time of wandering in the cold in fear and hunger, I realized the importance of helping people when they are in need and in trouble. I promised God that if I could live and be free, I would try to help those in need and do only good to others. I now know that this is the most important mission for people on earth and that God counts it as the highest commandment and achievement.

I did my sewing by the light shining into the barn from between the openings in the boards. The woman brought me food and I was happy, but it didn't last. Soon, the Germans were conducting house to house searches, entering the barns, and collecting food. I had to leave. The good woman let me stay until nightfall. She covered me with straw, in case the Germans looked into the barn. When it became dark, she came and told me that she had given the Germans vodka, eggs, and a lot of pig fat and they didn't bother to search her property. I thanked her with all my heart. I climbed down from the barn and left.

I went to Piekutowska, the woman who kept my cousin Faigele, to inquire. I hoped that maybe I would find Toiba. As it happened, Toiba arrived back from Pularie on that exact, same day. It seemed to me that our meeting was planned, as if some invisible force had made the arrangement. I was so happy to see Toiba alive and well. She told me that she had been making slippers. The people thought that she was Polish, until a young man from Lendowo-Budy arrived and told everybody that she was Jewish. At that point, she had to flee.

I looked out through Piekutowska's window. I saw a commotion in the village. Salkowski was walking with a horse and wagon, on his way to the woods. He was shouting: "Who wants to buy meat?" He took much pride in the fact that he had two dead Jews in the back of his wagon. They were the two tailors from Bransk, Shepst and Chaim.

Piekutowska told us that the tailors had kept a sewing machine in Dombrowski's attic, where they did a lot of sewing for the family and for others in the village. Although the sewing machine was only foot-operated, in Poland it was of great value. When the tailors decided to leave and take the sewing machine with them, the older son, who was greedy and wished to own the machine, called the Germans to come and kill the tailors.

When his younger brother found out that the Germans were coming, he tried to hide the tailors and covered them with hay. The Germans came, but they didn't find the tailors and left the house. The older brother ran after them. He told the Germans to look in the attic under the hay. They poked under the hay with their long blades. They killed the two tailors and pushed their bodies down the stairs. The blood covered the whole staircase.

Piekutowska warned that we would be next if we did not run away and escape to the bigger forests to search for the partisans. Toiba and I walked through the villages. We asked for directions to the larger forests. People advised us to go to the Lopienie Forest, which was near Sklody, Piekuty, and Kruczewo. This was not the biggest forest, but it was connected to other forests near Hodiszewo, such as the Bransk Forest, and even as far as the Bialowieza Forest. We walked until we found the Lopienie Forest.

It was spring. It was so peaceful; I could smell the perfumed scents of the land. The trees in blossom gave us shade from the sun and cover from the wind, and the air was fresh. We were resting under a tree, on the border of the village of Kruczewo when we heard screaming from the village. We listened and heard the shooting of firearms and the sound of babies crying. We smelled smoke and we knew that something was burning. We waited until it was dark, and then we walked to a farm near the forest.

The farmer, Itchkowski, and his family were very upset. They gave us food and told us that now, they understood the meaning of Nazi rule. That day, the Germans had killed and burned an entire village of innocent Polish people. It was a real massacre. The Germans had been taking a truckload of Polish people to Germany for forced labor. The Polish AK ambushed the convoy. They killed all the Germans and set the people free. The next morning, a German SS group arrived. They surrounded Kruczewo, just because it happened to be the village closest to the part of the road where the ambush took place. The Germans put the entire population of the village – men, women, children, and babies – into a barn and burned it down with them inside. Whoever tried to escape was shot.

One badly wounded man, however, did manage to escape. He crawled until he reached Itchkowski's farm and told them what happened to the people of Kruczewo. When the farmer talked to us, he broke down in tears. He said, "The Germans began by killing the Jews, but now, when they don't have any Jews to kill, they are going to kill the Poles."

We left Itchkowski's farm and went back to Lopienie Forest. We walked deeper into the forest, into the thicker woods, where we met a group of ten Jews. They were a mixture of people from different towns, of different ages. There was a woman about 30 years old named Chaike from Sokoly. There was Eidl's husband and his son. There were three youngsters from Wysokie whose name was Wrobel. Their father was a tailor. The older Wrobel boy was 20, his sister Sarah, 18, and their little brother, a boy of eight. There was a girl named Mirka from Lapy, and Toiba's mother, Sorche (Sarah Goldberg) Tabak, with her three-year-old son, Hershele Tabak.

Sorche told us about her life in this forest and the scare she had when her three-year-old son got lost. Sorche would go into the villages at night to collect food. It was difficult for her to carry the boy, so she would wait until he was asleep and then leave him overnight in an empty barn. In the morning, she would come back with some food to collect him.

One morning, when she came to get her son, he was not there. She asked the owner of the barn, but nobody had seen the little boy. Sorche looked for him in the forest. She came across a deaf and dumb shepherdess who took her to the Soltys, and he gave the boy back to her.

I heard the child talking about this episode; he was badly shaken and distressed. He woke up and didn't see his mother. He was afraid that she had left him for good. He went to look for her, first to the river, then to the forest. On the road a wagon stopped. He described a German who asked him what he was doing alone in the forest. Hershele told the man that his father had been killed and his mother had gone to look for food. The German told the shepherdess to take him to the Soltys. Now Hershele was back with his mother. He was very alert, with a mind like an adult. When the group was talking, the little boy cautioned the grown-ups to lower their voices, because somebody would hear and kill all of them.

Sorche was glad that Toiba and I had found her. She asked us to go and collect food for all of us, because it was very hard for her to walk and carry the boy as well. Toiba and I said that we would go. We left the camping place at sundown and walked towards the villages. I was afraid that we would get lost and not find the way back when we returned in the middle of the night, so we made signs all the way with stones and sticks. We put a large stone at the edge of the forest.

We came to a village named Lizanka, where the people looked at us in wonder. They asked how is it that we looked so well and appeared happy, when all the Jews they saw were frightened and pale. They told us that a few days ago a woman from Lapy and her daughter, Mirka's mother and sister, had been burned alive by the Germans in any empty shed at the end of this village.

The village people gave us food and we went back to the Lopienie Forest, to Sorche and the other Jews. Each morning, we went to the river to fetch water, and then we cooked potato soup. One morning, while we were cooking our soup, we suddenly heard a loud noise and commotion. We stopped talking and quickly extinguished the fire. We all felt such fright; we were sure that death was knocking at the door, and they were coming for us. It must be the Germans, or even the AK, who also killed Jews. We listened. How relieved we were when we heard Russian being spoken! We saw a group of 15 men with guns, one of them carrying a heavy machine gun, approaching us, and looked closer. It was true; they really were the Russian partisans!

WITH THE PARTISANS

Toiba Tabak recognized Wanka Smyrnov, who had been with her in the group near the Bransk Forest. Wanka was very happy to see Toiba again. He told her that after the shoot-out with the Germans near Bransk, he and the others kept looking for Toiba, her sister Feigale, and Stella, but could not find them. They crossed the Bug River, and not far from Treblinka, they met another group of Russians. They had joined together into one group, and now they were coming back to this part of the forest.

Most of the Russians were prisoners of war who had managed to jump off the trains in which they were being sent to prison or concentration camps. Wanka described the members of the group to us; some of them were real bandits – robbers and killers. The two worst bandits were Grishka, who carried the heavy machine gun, and Nicholai. These two robbed, raped, and killed, terrorizing the area around Treblinka, and the rest of the group just followed their lead.

Although some of the men in the group were killers, others were not bad, considering the circumstances. There was Paul Rasin, who thought of himself as a commander and liked to be fair. He was a good singer, and everybody liked him. His best friends were

Washka (Waska) Wierszynin, Pietka, and Nicholai Zygan. There were three Ukrainian men: Fyodor and Szewcrenko, who were educated, and Zahar, who shouted a lot, but was not dangerous. The others were Nichodem, Wolodka (Woloda), Wasniushka, Aloshka, and Nicholai the kolkhoznik. We called Nicholai the *kolkhoznik* because he had worked on a government farm in Russia. He told us that instead of working, he would hide under bundles of straw whenever he had the chance. Aloshka and Nicholai the kolkhoznik were very nice.

Wanka thought that it would be best if we went into hiding with the Jews in the Bransk Forest, because some of the men in his group were real killers. When the farmers would not open their doors to them, refused to give them food, or informed the Germans of their whereabouts, they would kill entire families and set fire to the farms. The villages around Bransk were populated by White Russian farmers who carried out the Germans' orders even more thoroughly than the Polish farmers. When Jews came to them, begging for a piece of bread, they would tie them up and take them to the Germans to be killed. For that reason, the Jews from Bransk were hiding in the forest. They did not get their food by begging, but rather, by going into a barn at night and killing a pig or a sheep, which they took back to the forest to cook. Even the Germans were careful not to come into this forest too often, because they knew that these Jews had guns.

Wanka explained to us that even in the Bransk Forest, we would not be completely safe from the Russian atrocities. But he told us not to worry, because he and his friend, Washka Wierszynin, promised to protect us. Wanka said that we should agree to his offer to take us to the place where the Jews were hiding in the Bransk Forest. We knew that we had no chance of survival on our own. The Polish AK or some other bandits would inform the Germans about us and they would come to kill us. We considered our situation: how unprotected we were, and how long we had waited to meet up with the partisans. For us, the offer to travel with the Russians was a must. Five of the younger Jews from the group were also permitted to join us.

When night fell, we all walked away from the Lopienie Forest, in the direction of the Hodiszewo Forest, where we set up a camp. Toiba Tabak and I kept very busy, doing everyone's laundry, mending clothes, and cooking meals for the group. One afternoon after dinner, everyone went their separate ways. Some members of the group were resting under the trees, some went for a walk, and others were engaged in discussion. Toiba and I were walking in the forest when we saw a group of ten men coming towards us with machine guns on their shoulders. We went back to our camp and whispered to Wanka Smyrnov what we had seen. We knew that Wanka was the best in dangerous situations; he never lost his cool. Now, he acted responsibly and rescued all of us.

Wanka walked towards the oncoming group with his automatic gun in his hand. He gave a command in Russian, told the leader of the group to come forward and the others to stay behind. He told them that they were surrounded and that he had been sent by his *Combrig* [commander] to meet them. Zahar, from our group, was so frightened that he started running around, shouting: "Everybody, get ready to fight, get ready!"

Wanka and the leader of the other group – who were members of the Polish AK – exchanged identity papers. Wanka put down the name of our group as "Brigade No. 1" and ordered the AK men to walk down the path where Grishka was situated with his heavy machine gun. Wanka wanted them to see how well-armed our group was. The Polish group left and we all breathed easier. We were happy that the sudden confrontation had ended peacefully.

A Polish man came to the forest to sell us vodka. He talked to the Russians and told them that they should join the Polish AK group, because both groups have a common enemy: the Germans. He said that in his opinion, the only obstacle to their unity was the Jews, and that the Russians should get rid of them. After that, the Russians began to act strangely; they began to talk in secret.

That night, the Russians called a meeting and announced that the Jews in the group were not allowed to attend. Toiba and I waited outside in the dark, anxious to hear news. When it was over, Wanka and Washka (Waska) came over to us. They were distressed and disgusted and told us to dress quietly and quickly, that we had to leave immediately, because the other Russians were planning to kill all the Jews in our group later that night. The four of us, Wanka Smyrnov, Washka Wierszynin, Toiba Tabak, and I, got dressed and left the place in a great hurry.

We walked all night on the road to the village of Lendowo-Budy. In the middle of the road, we came face-to-face with the two most notorious bandits from the village. But when they saw the Russians with guns in their hands, they were overcome by fear. They fell to their knees in fright and started to beg for mercy, thinking the Russians were going to kill them. Wanka and Washka told the bandits to stand up, that they were not going to kill them. They warned them to behave and not to kill any more innocent people. The two were extremely grateful that they were allowed to go free.

In the village we had no trouble walking into people's houses. The residents acted very friendly toward us and gave us good food. I saw that they had great respect for gun. We traveled together for a few days, after which we came back to the Lopienie Forest, to the same spot where we had camped before. There, we found a big surprise. Sitting under the trees were five of the Russians from our group.

Our surprise was even greater when we saw the sincere welcome they gave us when we arrived. They embraced us and showed genuine emotion, calling us *rebiata* [friends]. The five Russians were Fyodor, Zahar, Woloda, and the two quiet ones, Aloshka and Nicholai the kolkhoznik. The Russians told us what happened after we left the group in the Hodiszewo Forest. That same night, there was a lot of drinking and there were murders. Nicholai the kolkhoznik saw how Grishka robbed Chaike from Sokoly of her jewelry – a necklace, watch, and wedding ring. After that, Nicholai

Zygan shot her and some other Jews. Then they went to a Polish farm and killed the whole family.

After these murders, the Russian bandits went to a forest near Dominowo Stare. Some Poles followed them and informed the Germans of their whereabouts. The Germans surrounded the forest and the worst bandits from the group, Grishka with his machine gun, Nicolai Zygan, Nichodem, and some others were killed; the rest of them ran away in different directions.

The five Russians told us that they did not hate the Jews and that it was not true that the Polish AK would join up with the partisans. They had heard of a few Russians who did join the AK, but members of the AK had killed them in the Veliner Forest, where the AK had a hideout. The Russians knew that they could not trust the AK and were very happy to join us.

We continued walking during the night, back to the Hodiszewo Forest. There we met two young Jewish men from Bialystok and one older man, Jacob Fabricki, from Kolno. The Russians ordered these Jews to empty their pockets. They frisked them and took what little money and jewelry they had. Fabricki had a gold watch and secretly gave it to Toiba to hide. After the search, she gave it back to him.

Although the three Jews were treated with contempt by the Russians, they were glad to have met our group. They told us that they had built a bunker in this forest, where they slept at night, and that, during the day the day, they hid in the woods. They asked us if they could spend the days with our group because they felt safer with people who had guns. The three Jews would bring us potatoes. We had bread and fat, so we cooked and ate together. At night, they would go to sleep in their bunker. One night, we heard shots. In the morning, Fabricki came looking for his two friends. He told us that that night, it had been his turn to bring potatoes from the holes near the villages. When he returned, he found the bunker empty and no sign of the two boys. We understood that either the AK or bandits had ambushed and shot them near the bunker.

The next day, two young Polish men came into the forest and talked very politely to the Russians. They asked if the Russians had any money and whether they would like to buy some vodka. The Russians answered that they did have some money, and yes, they very much wanted to buy vodka. The Poles promised to deliver the vodka the following morning.

Early the next morning, Toiba and I went to the cooking area, which was some distance from the place where we slept. We made a fire and started to cook. Soon, the men woke up and came over to the fire to warm themselves while waiting for the food to be ready. In the meantime, they talked, discussing politics. Suddenly, there was shooting from the sleeping area, where we kept our guns.

Our panic was very great. None of us even thought of attempting to turn back to collect our guns, clothing and shoes, because the shooting came from that direction. We did not even think about our personal belongings. Our only concern was to save ourselves. We just ran and kept on running further away from the shooting, into the thicker bushes, where we finally were able to rest.

We saw Wanka Smyrnov coming towards us. He was furious with us all for being such cowards. He was the only one who didn't run away but shot back at the attackers. He crawled back to our camp on his hands and knees and collected the guns and ammunition. Wanka gave each one of us a gun, a rifle, or a hand grenade. He ordered us to go back and surround the bandits and shoot back at them. We followed Wanka, each one of us carrying a weapon ready to shoot. The tension was enormous. When we came closer, we saw smoke coming from our camping place. Our clothing and shoes were burning. There was no sign of the attackers.

The next morning, at dawn, we started walking from the Hodiszewo Forest to the Bransk Forest. It was a frosty autumn morning. A few of us, including me, walked barefoot. My feet were numb. The wheat in the fields had been cut down, and as we walked on for many kilometers over the stiff straw, I felt like I was walking on needles or sharp nails. The hard straw pierced the soles of my feet, causing enormous pain. Yet, in my mind, I was thankful that I was not alone and that I was in company with men who were not afraid, who carried guns and knew how to use them. Despite my painful feet, I felt comfortable and relaxed. I was neither frightened nor helpless.

On a Sunday evening, we arrived at a forest near a village and heard music playing. There was a party in the village; people were drinking and dancing. As soon as it got dark, Wanka Smyrnov, Washka Wierszynin, and a few others who wore boots, went towards the village. The rest of us, who were barefoot, sat down to wait for them to come back. We heard shots being fired in the village. My first impulse was to pray that the men would come back safely. After a long wait that seemed like forever, they returned, bringing boots for all of us who were barefoot. We all put on our newly acquired boots and continued on our way.

We walked mostly during the nights. In the daytime, we rested in the forest. On a beautiful day, early in autumn, when the sun was shining and the breeze brought us the pleasant fragrance of the forest air, we were sitting under the trees at the edge of the forest, close to a road when a farmer came along and started talking to the Russians.

The farmer was really distressed. He spoke about the Germans, saying that fighting is one thing, but killing hundreds of thousands of innocent civilians, men, women, and children, is murder. The farmer had been present during the massacre of people from Ciechanowiec, my hometown. He saw how the Germans shot the entire Jewish population of the town: men, women and children, for no reason. They were taken to a large, prearranged pit in a forest where they were stripped naked, shot, and buried.

In the middle of the conversation, we saw two Germans in uniform, with rifles on their shoulders, walking near us on the road towards the village. Wanka took his automatic rifle and aimed at the Germans. Then I watched the farmer take hold of Wanka's hand to prevent him from shooting. He started to kiss Wanka's hands and begged him not to shoot those Germans. He did not do this because he loved the Germans, but because each German was valued at 80 Polish people. If these two Germans were to be killed, then 160 Polish people from the nearest village would be shot in retaliation. Wanka listened to the farmer and lowered his rifle.

Wanka was the best shot in our group. When we needed food, he would shoot a pigeon in mid-flight; we would cook it and have a good meal. In warlike situations, in times of danger, Wanka was the best. His weakness was that he was an alcoholic. He could drink like a fish without any limits. Then he would start shooting and we would all run for cover. Luckily, when he was drunk, he became blind and would shoot without seeing us. Then he would fall asleep. When he woke up and we told him of his behavior, he would cry and apologize, and promise not to drink any more. But we knew that his promise would last only until the next time.

SPARK OF HOPE

We kept on walking through fields and forests, until we came to the Bransk Forest. There, we met the rest of the Russian partisans: Paul Rasin, Pietka, Wolodia, Zahar, Fyodor, and Wasil.

About 70 Jews were hiding in bunkers in the Bransk Forest. Some of these were families, others were groups of single men and women. They were very careful not to walk around during the day, but at night they felt safe, because Germans never came into the forest after dark. At night, each group would make a fire and cook their meals. They would sing together, and often visited each other.

When our group arrived, we went to the bunker of Chaim Finkelstein and his family. Chaim was blond, tall, well-built, and smart. His wife, Matel, was short and friendly, with blond, curly hair. Matel was a good housewife. Even in the forest, she cooked tasty meals. When we came to their cooking place, the Finkelsteins greeted us in friendship and offered us a good, hot meal. Their older daughter, Shoshka, was a pretty, lively 17-year-old, who was always smiling. The 15-year-old younger daughter, Chanale (Chana) was a sweet girl. Their son, Avramele (Avraham), was 13 years old.

Hiding in the same bunker with the Finkelstein family were two brothers from Bransk, Yossel and Itzik Broida. Yossel was 22 years old. He was tall, blond, and courageous. His brother, who was about 18 years old, was very handsome and sang beautiful songs. A young man named Velvel Halperin, who was also tall and handsome, was another occupant of the Finkelstein's bunker. He was Shoshka's boyfriend and was readily accepted as a member of the family and brought food for the whole family.

Water accumulated in the bunker, so the occupants made a drainage hole. Each night, they filled many buckets of water from the drainage hole and spilled them out into the forest. In spite of this problem, they thought that their bunker was safer than most, because the owner of that part of the forest was an honest man, who would not inform the Germans of their presence.

The next night, we visited another family, a woman named Gittel Rubinstein and her children. Gittel's only son, Moshe, was 17 years old; he was a fine, gentle young man. The oldest daughter, Kikla, was 20 years old. The second daughter, Bobehe, was 16 years old and very beautiful. The youngest, Sonia, was 13 years old and an invalid. She could not talk properly, she walked slowly and crookedly and was very scared of thunderstorms. When there was a German roundup in the forest, Gittel never left; she would tell her other children to run away and hide, but she and Sonia never left the forest. They hid in the thickest bushes and watched the Germans walking past them with their guns, searching for partisans and Jews.

We visited another bunker, which was occupied by Haim Velvel Pribut, a courageous young man who lived there with Moshe Janczeman and Moshe Oskard. A bit further on was David Edlak's bunker, where he lived with two Jews from Bialystok, a solicitor named Olek Grzebin and a writer named Mattis. Olek and Mattis had frozen feet, because their boots had been stolen by murderous gangs. Jacob Fabricki from Kolno, who came all the way to the Bransk Forest with our Russian group, also found a place to stay in

David Edlak's bunker. David Olenski promised to help provide David Edlak with food in exchange for taking in these three extra people.

We met and were introduced to the three Olenski brothers: David, Avraham and Shlomo. We found them to be very capable young men. The three brothers helped provide food for many of the hungry people in the forest. Staying with the Olenskis in their bunker were their cousins Dina and her brother Jacob, and Jacob's wife, Rivka. Jacob was tragically killed on a mission to bring food to the partisans hiding in the forest.

Berl Pelchowitz, Symcha Pam and his sister-in-law Brocha, Brocha's father – a tailor – and Leibl Trus, a courageous young man from Bransk all lived in a bunker together. Another bunker housed Joheved Golda, a photographer from Bransk, and her brother, Velvel. A beautiful girl from Wolomin came to the river and was found by the boys. She went to stay in a bunker with Israel Brenner and Avraham Olenski.

A young girl originally from Kovno, Lithuania, Luba Frank, found her way to our group in the forest. Luba Frank, together with two of her cousins had jumped out of a train that was on its way to Treblinka. Her cousins had been shot and Luba was now alone in the world. She did not speak Polish, only Lithuanian, and begged for food from shepherds. When she saw Germans on the road, she would pick up a stick and pretend to be a shepherdess. Duvche Olenski heard about this young girl and sent two men to rescue her and bring her to the group in the forest. They made it back to the Bransk Forest, where she joined one of the Jewish groups.

Two brothers from Bransk, Moshe and Samuel Kleinot, were hiding with Samuel Rechelson in a bunker in a Polish cemetery. Benjamin Pribut, his sister, Esterke (Esther) the redhead, Rachel Cheslak, Jakob Rubin, and many more Jews, were hiding in a bunker near the village of Zwirydy.

In a separate bunker, near the village of Hodiszewo, Chaim Wrobel, who was known as the *Kewlaker,* was hiding with Stella Szcrecranska, who was nine years old. "Little Stella," as she was called, was born in Bialystok, on the Polish side of the city. Her father was a chemist, and her family spoke only Polish. Little Stella and her parents were on a deportation train on the way to Treblinka, when her mother wrapped her in a towel and threw her out the window.

Some Poles, who were walking alongside the train tracks, looking for money or boots on the bodies of dead Jews who had been shot or accidentally killed while jumping from the passing trains, found Little Stella alive among the dead Jews. They picked her up and took her to the priest in Hodiszewo. That day, Chaim the Kewlaker came to the priest for food. The priest gave Chaim some food and gave Little Stella to him, telling him to take care of her so Chaim took her to his bunker.

The people we met in the Bransk Forest told me that before we arrived, a group of 15 Russian bandits had caused them a great deal of suffering. These Russians had been terrorizing all the Jews in the Bransk Forest. They stole all of the food and clothing from the bunkers and raped all the women and girls they could find. They gang-raped them, all 15 of the Russians standing in queues for a turn. When we came to the forest with our own group of Russians, the worst of these bandits were dead.

We had discussions with the remaining Russian bandits about their thoughts regarding the Jews. They had a bad opinion of us. I stood up and explained to them that we are all human and that no one should judge other people by their nationalities, but rather, only as individuals. I said that nobody can be responsible for the actions of others, only for their own.

I was never jealous or greedy. When I cooked, I always tried to fairly divide the food. A good relationship was established between the Russians and the Jews in the Bransk Forest. Paul Rasin was the commander of the military group, to which all the young Jewish men and women also belonged. Chaim Finkelstein was a deputy leader of the family group. Duvche Olenski and his brothers were the overall leaders of the family group. In the forest Duvche was known by all as the *Kaiser*.

During the days we were careful, always sitting together in groups. At night, we would make a big fire, cook our food, eat, and sing beautiful Russian war songs.

Together, our group of Russians and Jews discussed the possibility of a German attack on our forest. Washka Wierszynin taught us how to escape a German blockade. He was so clever that he could find his way in the dark, in the thickest bushes. I was really upset, because I knew that in the forest, I was hopeless. I had no sense of direction; I just followed the others. So, I found myself talking to God and asking Him for help. I knew that by myself, without Divine help, I would not be able to escape from the Germans.

THE GERMANS ATTACK

It was winter 1943. The trees and the entire forest were covered with snow and frost. We had seen and felt the warmth of the Jewish bunkers, so the Russians decided to do the same. They dug out underground shelters, and each group of eight or ten people had a separate shelter. It was wonderfully warm inside the bunker. We used a tree as the door to our bunker which I shared with Toiba, Wanka Smyrnov, Washka Wierszynin, Nicholai the *Kolkhoznik*, Aloshka, Zahar, Fyodor, and some others. During the days, we stayed in our shelter, and each night we went out to light a fire and cook our food.

On one particular night we cooked together with Gittel Rubinstein and her family. Later, we went to sleep in our warm shelter and I dreamed that I saw my mother. In my dream also saw a man shooting at Washka Wierszynin. I saw him fall, I heard the loud bang of the gun, and woke up screaming in fright. All my companions woke up and asked me what happened. I told them that I had dreamed that I heard a shot. They grumbled and complained that I was disturbing their sleep. I felt guilty and could not sleep any more.

Whilst I was tossing and turning, trying to get back to sleep, I heard footsteps on top of our bunker and called out to my comrades again. Some of the Russians among us answered crossly that a dog running through the forest must have made the noise, but Wanka wanted to make sure. He moved closer to the entrance of the bunker with his loaded automatic gun in his hand. He carefully pulled aside the small tree hiding the opening, and, in the semi-darkness, he saw two human shadows. He pulled the trigger and shot the Germans. They were wounded but managed to throw a hand grenade into our bunker. Wanka caught the hand grenade and threw it back into the woods and we heard a loud explosion. After that, the battle began.

The Germans let loose a barrage of bullets and grenades. Our bunker became a battlefield; they were firing at us from all sides. We heard machine gun fire and the Germans shouting, just like on the front line. A hundred Germans with machine guns and explosives surrounded our bunker. We only had three rifles, three pistols, two hand grenades, and a small amount of ammunition. Wanka was shooting, but in response to every one of his shots, the Germans fired hundreds of bullets from their machine guns. They were also using grenades to flush out the other partisans from their hiding places. The air was filled with the sounds of gunfire and explosions. It was clear that we would be defeated; that we would inevitably perish in that smoke-filled hole.

My first thought was to keep on shooting so that we could stay alive for a little while longer. On the other hand, if no shots were fired from our bunker, perhaps the Germans would not throw in grenades and bury us. The fighting continued for several hours until we saw rays of sunshine through the tree covering the entrance of our bunker. Wanka ordered me to give him the rifle and reload his automatic gun. I gave the gun to Aloszka to put in the bullets, but he answered that he couldn't do it. I saw that his hands were shaking. He knelt on the ground and prayed to God for help. Zahar was lamenting. "Lubka," he said, "it's so hard to die when I can see the beautiful sunshine through the tree." I put the bullets in the gun and gave it back to Wanka. I took the rifle and fired. The rifle ran out of bullets. As I was reloading it, I turned in fright. I saw Wanka, shouting loudly from the entrance of the bunker to the Germans, "*Urra! Urra!* [Kill the Germans! Kill the Germans!]" I looked at him, thinking he was screaming because he had lost his mind.

When our ammunition was nearly finished, I saw Wanka turn to us with his gun in his hand. He ordered us to climb out of the bunker and threatened to shoot anyone who did not obey him and leave the relative safety of the bunker. Instinct told us that to climb out of the bunker, when the Germans on top were shooting, was like going to meet death with open arms. Inside, we were protected from the bullets. But the life-threatening command from Wanka was so powerful that, without thinking, each one of us climbed out in turn.

My turn came to climb out. I pulled my jacket behind me through the opening and then I was outside. I heard the Germans shouting at me, "*Halt!*" Hundreds of bullets from their machine guns burst past my head. I was so engulfed in the smoke from the gunpowder that I was sure that I had been shot. Maybe I would soon be dead, but I still had an irresistible urge to run for cover deeper into the safety of the thicker bushes. I ran.

I couldn't see the Germans anymore. I stopped and touched my body, my back, looking for blood. I touched my hair. It was shorn by the bullets and smelled burnt. I kept on running. I saw barefoot footprints in the white snow and understood that it was safer to run barefoot, because boots make a lot of noise. I took off my boots and ran barefoot. I devoted all my attention to following the footprints in the snow.

After I ran a few kilometers, the footprints ended. I stopped and looked. I saw a road with a forest on the other side. I crossed the road and joined my companions from the bunker. The only one missing from our group was Washka Wierszynin. Later, we found out that the Germans had shot and killed him, just like I saw in my dream.

I could not feel my feet; they were frozen and numb. I remembered that I had learned in school that the best remedy for frostbitten feet is to rub them with snow. I sat for hours, rubbing my feet with snow, until I felt some sensation. I put on my boots, but without a rag or a piece of cloth to wrap around them inside the boots, my feet were terribly cold.

When we ran from our bunker, the other partisans did the same. Those from our bunker who were killed were Washka Wierszynin and Haim Velvel Pribut's brother, Josef Pribut, who was 14 years old. The others managed to run away. After a few days, all of us went back to the Bransk Forest. Our meeting place was always Gittel Rubinstein's bunker. We would look into Gittel's bunker from the outside and ask her, "Grandma, are you alive?" She would always answer, "I must outlive that murderer, Hitler. Only then will I die, and not before."

COUNTERACTIONS

Although at that time our group of Russians did not have any connection with the real partisans, they tried to act responsibly. They really wished to do something to help Russia win the war. They loved their troubled country and hated the German murderers who had killed so many civilians and made slaves of all the others. They were also concerned about what would happen when they were liberated. Would they be charged with desertion? They knew that there were groups of real partisans who had connections to Moscow near the large Bialowieza Forest, but how could they find them?

In the meantime, Rasin was trying to organize the group as best he could. Woloda, an older, educated man, was chosen as secretary to keep records. Rasin picked the younger Jews and Russians to carry out a counteraction project. I was ordered to participate in the mission, along with the Russian doctor, who helped me cook and carry the pots and pans.

Our assigned project was to cut down all the telephone poles on the way to Bransk and Ciechanowiec, the direct line on the main road to Warsaw. All the telephone wires were taken out and the poles were chopped down. We moved further on. All I knew was that we walked and walked without any sleep for many days and nights.

One night, we stopped for a rest. I leaned my head on a stone and fell asleep with such delight. But soon Rasin woke us up and ordered us to move and march on again. I was very sad, and sleep deprived but we had to obey. We walked in single file, one after the other. The doctor walked behind me with the *kocholoks*. These were army pots with wire handles. Suddenly, I felt somebody push me. I woke up and wondered where I was. I soon realized that I had been walking in my sleep. I was frightened and I tried to keep my mind occupied with thoughts to stay awake and not fall asleep anymore.

It started to rain. We were wet, but we kept on walking until we came to the Veliner Forest. When we arrived, we found a huge tree, as big as a mansion. The tree had grown like a roof; its branches reached the ground, and 100 people could fit inside under the branches. Inside the tree, it was lovely, warm and dry. I was very happy that we finally were able to rest.

Suddenly, there was a great deal of shooting from all sides, aimed in our direction. We returned fire but had to run out from under the shelter of the huge tree, back into the forest and the rain. We ran through trees, fields, and meadows until we arrived safely back in the Bransk Forest. Later, we learned that the tree in the Blonie Forest was a hideout for the Polish AK. They had greeted us with their shooting.

We needed food and arms, so Rasin organized for another group of Jews and Russians to go on a mission. The plan was to attack some Germans who occupied a mansion in Wilkowo, not far from Bransk, and to collect a few machine guns and some food. On the way to Wilkowo, the group stopped at a Polish farmhouse where the owner gave them some food and vodka. When the Russians were a bit drunk and in a happy mood, they talked. They boasted what big heroes they were going to be, that they were going to help the Polish get rid of the Germans.

The farmer belonged to the AK and informed his people of the Russians' intentions. When the group left the farm, they were ambushed by the AK, who fired at them with machine guns. One man from our group was killed and five others were wounded. The man who was killed was a Jew, 24-year-old Shaye Tabak from Wyszonki. Shlomo Olenski and Moshe Kleinot were wounded. More seriously wounded were Pietka, Zygan, and Aloshka.

In the forest, we heard the loud noise of a horse and wagon arriving. The survivors of the group were bringing the wounded men back to our camp. They were shouting out to us to help them take the men out of the wagon. All of us, including me, tended to the wounded. Their blood was still flowing, and they were as pale as white chalk. Their moans chilled my heart. They told us that they had been ambushed by a group of Polish AK and when they tried to run, a machine gun cut them down in the dark.

The wounded were lying bleeding all night. In the morning a farmer and his wife came riding on their way to church. The Russian partisans aimed their rifles at the couple and told them to take the wounded to the Bransk Forest. They were placed on the ground and Rasin told the farmer and his wife to go on to church. We put the bandaged men back into our wagon and Rasin and the Russian doctor took the wounded to the farm of a friendly White Russian family, where the doctor treated them until their wounds were healed.

It was early spring 1944. There was positive news of the progress of the war. The Germans were retreating, and the Russians were advancing. The Russians in our group were restless so they decided to walk to the large Bialowieza Forest, near Hajnowka, to find the real partisans. They also believed that after they had cut down the telephone poles, and the farmer had seen our hideout, the Bransk Forest was no longer safe. They had heard rumors that the Germans were planning to attack the forest again so all of the Russians, except Wanka, walked away in the direction of the Bialowieza Forest.

It was a radiant spring morning, yet I felt sadder and lonelier than ever. Although there still were a few Jewish families in the forest, I did not want to impose on them. I sat alone and thought about my situation. A deathlike stillness filled the air. Suddenly, I saw the sky opening and a red ball of fire falling down onto the trees. I looked at that red ball of fire and thought that the whole sky was falling right on top of me. I heard a loud explosion, a deafening boom. I was lucky again; the fireball hit the ground only a few meters from my hiding place. I stood up and carefully looked through the bushes. There was a huge deep hole in the ground, as big as a grand mansion. About ten minutes later, I heard a car stopping. Three Germans dressed in civilian clothing had come to inspect the damage from the missile.

Another tragic incident occurred a few months later which affected us all and reminded us that despite the news from the front, danger was still present all the time. Our lives continued to remain hanging on a thread. It was approaching winter and not far from the Bransk Forest, a group of eight young Jews from Bialystok had built a bunker. A Polish farmer told Duvche (David) Olenski what had occurred: the Polish AK discovered the group of Jews, threw hand-grenades into their bunker, and killed them all.

Duvche Olenski insisted that we must go and bury the dead and say mourners' kaddish for them. He was a man of integrity, but this was a very dangerous thing to do, especially since we were all concerned that their footprints in the snow would leave a trail to our bunker, and we would be the next targets. Nevertheless, Duvche Olenski insisted that it was the right thing to do and ordered two men to accompany him on the unpleasant task. Chaim the Kewlaker, Hershel the Drayster, and David Olenski set out to give the victims a dignified Jewish burial. They risked their lives to travel some ten kilometers or more away while we remained in our bunker and worried about their safety.

When they safely reached the victims in the bunker, there was an awful stench in the air, and they heard moaning. They found one girl still alive, but badly wounded. A grenade had blown off part of her leg, and it was infected. The men rescued the girl and brought her out of the bunker. Hershel the Drayster carried her on his back for many kilometers to a Polish farm, together with the other two men. Duvche demanded that the farmer take care of the girl and get medical assistance for her. He gave the farmer some money for medicine and for his efforts.

A miracle occurred on the men's journey back home. It began snowing heavily; all their footsteps were covered up by the new snowfall and they arrived back to the Bransk forest safely. We later learned that the girl's name was Edria Katz, and that she was from Bialystok. Eventually, Edria recovered from her wounds, and Hershel married her. After the war, they went to live in Mandate of Palestine.

WITH THE JEWS FROM BRANSK

Life continued in the Bransk forest over the winter. I stayed in a bunker with a few Jews from Bransk: Haim Velvel Pribut, Moshe Janczeman and Moshe Oskard, along with my cousin Toiba Tabak, and Wanka Smyrnov. We spent the days in the bunker and went out to cook at night. We agreed that each night, a different pair of people would do the cooking. It was very cold, snowing and dark. Nobody wanted to go outside, except Moshe Oskard and me.

We took two empty buckets, a small bag of potatoes and a piece of pig fat. Moshe walked ahead, and I followed. We walked in pitch darkness until we came to the river, where we drew two buckets of water. We carried the water for a kilometer to David Edlak's bunker and shouted to the people in the bunker to come out and join us.

David and Fabricki also came out to cook. The other two residents of the bunker, the solicitor, Olek Grzebin, and Mattis, the scholar from Bialystok, had already given up on life itself. They put their hands outside the bunker and answered that it was too cold; they would rather eat raw potatoes. Maybe they didn't come out because their legs were frozen. We gathered sticks and made a big fire. I peeled the potatoes and cooked them with the pig fat. We took a full bucket of hot potato soup back to our bunker and shared it with everyone. The next night, nobody wanted to go outside to cook in the bitter cold. I thought that it was very important that we not become lazy. After that, Moshe Oskard and I went out to do the cooking every night.

One morning, Moshe Rubinstein jumped into our bunker and stayed all day. He told us that the night before, he had taken his 16-year-old sister Bobehe to visit another bunker and that he was on his way back to his mother. Bobehe was restless, Moshe said. For weeks, she had begged her mother to let her go to the other bunker, where the young people had a good time together and lived in a happier atmosphere than in her mother's bunker. While we were talking, we heard the sounds of gunfire and explosions in the distance.

Moshe left and Haim Velvel Pribut asked me to come with him to visit the bunker where Moshe Rubinstein had taken Bobehe. I agreed and we left as soon as the sun went down and walked for a few kilometers in the dark, until we reached the bunker. Haim Velvel shouted into the bunker. He called the names of all those who lived there, but there was no answer. We could only hear insects crawling. I knew that something terrible had happened.

Haim Velvel Pribut did not understand why his friends had all vanished. He decided to go to Hershel Shepak's bunker, which was nearby, to get information. It was already daybreak when we arrived at the other bunker and met the occupants: Berl Pelchowitz, 25 years old; Symcha Pam, 28 years old; Brocha, aged 26; her father, Hershel Shepak, a 50-year-old tailor; and a young boy, Leibl Trus, aged 18.

The people in Hershel Shepak's bunker told us what had happened in the other bunker. A Polish man from Swirydy, Frank Dniester, informed the Germans where those Jews were hiding, and the Germans came and killed them all. They threw hand grenades and burning straw into the bunker. The irritating smoke forced all the Jews to go outside, and then the Germans easily shot them with their machine guns. Among those killed were Moshe Kleinot, 22 years old; Leibl Paw, aged 25, Benjamin Pribut, aged 18; Rachel Cheslak, aged 18; and Bobehe Rubinstein, aged 16.

After hearing what had happened to those beautiful young people, we were frightened and depressed. We thought, *How can we tell Mule Kleinot about the death of his beloved brother, Moshe? How will we tell Esterke, the redhead, of the death of her only protector, her beloved older brother Benjamin Pribut and, especially, how can we tell Gittel Rubinstein about the death of her jewel, her beautiful daughter, Bobehe?*

Brocha and the five others from Hershel's bunker all knew how hopeless the situation was; they also were afraid and distressed. The bunker felt unsafe. We all went out to hide in the forest for the day. At nightfall, Haim Velvel and I left the group and walked away, sad and troubled, back to the Bransk Forest, to the bunker where the rest of our group were hiding.

Gittel Rubinstein had been a happy woman. She would always sing while she cooked. But when she was told the terrible news, she lamented the death of her beloved Bobehe. She asked, "Why? Why? Why is my beautiful daughter dead and the stupid invalid Sonia still alive?"

One early morning, when Moshe Janczeman went out of our bunker for fresh air, he saw two Polish men watching him. He knew them from Bransk. They promised to bring him food and he believed them. Moshe was prepared to stay in the bunker and wait for their help, but Haim Velvel and I thought differently. We had just come back from the visit to the other bunker and were still shaken by the deaths of our friends. The news about the betrayal by the informant Frank Dniester, their supposed Polish friend, made us wonder if we could trust anyone anymore.

Wanka Smyrnov also reminded us of what had happened when he trusted a man's promise regarding our bunker; a few months earlier, when Yossel Broida and Velvel Halperin came to visit us, they saw a man observing our bunker. They advised Wanka to go out and talk to the man, and he did so. Wanka told the man that he knew that his name was Adamczyk and that his house in Bransk was at the end of the street. Wanka said that if Adamczyk informed the Germans of our hiding place, other Russians would take revenge. Adamczyk solemnly swore that he would not inform the Germans, but a week later, he was the one who came and showed the Germans where our bunker was located.

Finally, after lengthy discussions, we made a decision to move out of our bunker. We moved into an empty, broken bunker, deeper in the forest. That night, our entire group went to sleep in a big, empty hole. Only Toiba and I were awake. We had a huge fright when we saw a pair of eyes looking at us in the dark. We soon realized it was a fox, so we quickly made a fire, and it ran away. The foxes were accustomed to coming to this bunker to dig out dead bodies. David Edlak later told us the story of that bunker. When David ran away from the Bransk ghetto, he came to the forest together with 27 young Jews. They were the ones who built that bunker. They bought food from the farmers and did not let David stay with them because he did not have any money. David built himself a little bunker not far away from them, and every night he came to them to beg for some food.

One day, when David was in his little bunker, he heard shooting, but he thought that the noise was from farmers cutting trees. In the evening, he went to the big bunker to get some food and found all 27 of the young men dead, killed by the Germans. David, who was poor and helpless, was the only one of that group who survived the war.

Much later, we seriously discussed this fact and concluded that it looked as if God especially chose the ones who were the least able to survive, so that no one would boast that they survived on their own merit. Wanka Smyrnov also reminded us of the three Jews whom we had met in the Hodiszewo Forest. Two of them were young, strong and clever, but the third, Fabricki, was older and helpless. The two young, clever men were killed, yet that helpless Fabricki survived the war. When Fabricki's glasses broke, he picked up all the broken pieces and explained that after the war, it would cost him less to make a new pair of glasses. That was at a time when we had lost all hope of ever getting free. We lived from day to day and heard rumors that Moscow was occupied by the Germans.

Toiba and I did the laundry for the group, using soap that we collected from the Poles, who in turn got it from the Germans. The soap was formed into small, white pieces and on each piece, the letters RJF were stamped. Later, people told us that the soap was made from the fat of the killed Jews and that RIF means *Rein Juden Fat* [pure Jewish fat].

I used to wash the shirts for the entire group. The only one who did not let me wash his shirts was Moshe Oskard. He never liked to be given anything by anyone. Moshe arrived in the Bransk forest barefoot and did not own any shoes. When the men from the Bransk Forest gave him a pair of shoes, he refused to take them. He was a shoemaker by trade, and an expert in sewing the upper parts of shoes. Once we had animal skin, so Moshe cut a pair of moccasins for himself from the skin, and those were the shoes that he wore.

Moshe Oskard had a friend, a Polish farmer, whom we called the "Grandfather." This farmer used to bake bread to sell. He sold it at a reduced price only to Moshe Oskard, because he knew him to be a very honest person. We had bread, but nothing else. Haim Velvel Pribut decided that he would go to bring us meat and fat. He left alone one evening with no gun. He carried only a torch, and I wondered what he would do with it.

After two days, Haim Velvel returned with a killed piglet on his shoulders. He told us that he had gone to a farm on the other side of Bransk. In order to get there, he crossed over a bridge because he liked to cover his tracks. While he was on the bridge, he saw a couple walking towards him. Instead of panicking and running away, he walked closer to them and shone his torch into their faces. They covered themselves and Haim Velvel walked away in the darkness. Haim knew that his mission was dangerous. If he'd been caught, he would have been killed, yet he took courage and hoped for the best. He risked his life to bring food for his friends, whom he liked and wished to help. We cooked and ate the food that Haim Velvel brought us and gave thanks to that courageous boy, who was only 18 years old.

The only one who refused to eat was Moshe Oskard. He claimed that he did not like to use people; he had too much pride. Oskard's cousin, Moshe Janczeman, was the opposite. He never wanted to do anything, but he was always ready to eat when others prepared the food. He acted with superiority towards others, as if everybody owed him something.

It was spring 1944. In the Bransk Forest, we no longer used the bunker; we lived out in the open. The trees sheltered us from the wind and rays of sunshine penetrated through the branches to warm us. It was pleasant and the air was fresh. I kept busy and had no time to worry or think unpleasant thoughts. Despite the daily uncertainty, I was happy and grateful to God for being alive.

The Finkelstein family established themselves nearby. They kept their belongings under a tree. Whenever I had free time, I was at Finkelstein's place, where there was always some action. Matel would be washing and cooking, Shoshka would be laughing, Chaim would be joking, Avramele complaining, Itzik Broida singing, and Chanale asking her mother for food, not for herself, but for the two sick men who could not walk. I saw Chanale carrying a jug of soup and bread to Olek Grzebin and Mattis, who lived far away in David Edlak's bunker.

I asked Shoshka where they had kept all their parcels of linen and clothing until then. Shoshka told me that her father had a Polish friend in Bransk, a poor man with a bad reputation. But when her father, Chaim Finkelstein, decided to collect his linen, tablecloths, underwear, and eiderdowns, he just knocked at the man's window and the man gave him all the parcels. In contrast, another Jewish man from Bransk, Yosel Szpytalny, had a Polish friend with a blameless reputation. Josel gave his friend some clothing to hide.

One night, 22-year-old Yosel came to his friend to collect a pair of boots from the parcel. The friend told him to wait until he brought the boots from the barn. Instead of going to the barn, he went to call the police. They took Yosel to the Germans, who shot him.

I loved to visit the Finkelsteins and chat with Shoshka. One day we sat on her eiderdowns. The next day we both became extremely itchy and covered in awful hives. Perhaps there were bedbugs or maybe we were allergic to eiderdown? I became very worried. I thought, *What can I do about an itch, in the middle of a forest, with no ointment or help?* Shoshka called me aside and told me that she had some ointment that her father had received from a Polish doctor in Bransk. She asked me to help her to rub the ointment on her itchy body. Shoshka also let me use some of her ointment. After a few days, the itchiness disappeared.

One day, we were all at the Finkelsteins' place, when Paul Rasin and Nicholai Zygan suddenly appeared. They were very distressed and secretive. They called Velvel Halperin and Yossel Broida to approach them and began to talk secretly with them. We were all curious and moved closer to eavesdrop on their conversation.

Paul and Nicholai said that they and the other Russians had left the Bransk Forest, intending to walk to the Bialowieza Forest, where they would be able to meet the real partisans. Close to Bialowieza was a town called Hajnowka. There were small villages around Hajnowka, where some White Russian farmers lived. Our group of Russians arrived in one of those villages and inquired about the partisans.

Suddenly, our Russians were surrounded by armed uniformed men and ordered to hand over their guns and ammunition. They were told that their attackers were real Russian partisans under Combrig Martinov, of General Kaposta's unit. Martinov was from Moscow, a paratrooper with the rank of Major, in a uniform decorated with medals. He led a group of 50 partisans, some of whom carried machine guns. The partisans thought our group were German spies and threatened to shoot them.

Combrig Martinov told our men that once, in the Bialowieza Forest, his group had trusted a similar group, who pretended to be partisans, but in truth were *Wlasowces* [renegade army named after Andrej Vlassov] who worked for the Germans with the intention of finding and killing the real partisans. When everybody was asleep, the Wlasowces went and brought the Germans, who killed many of the partisans and their families.

The partisans did not want to take any more chances and said that they intended to kill our group. Paul Rasin told the Combrig that they could not possibly be spies, because they were living together with Jews in the Bransk Forest. That statement is what saved them. The partisans arrested eight of our men and sent Paul and Nicholai to bring them a few live Jews. If they did so, then the other eight men would be set free. When we heard this story, we were happy that we would soon be able to meet the real partisans. Yossel Broida and Velvel Halperin volunteered to go with Rasin and Nicholai.

A week later, as we were doing our daily tasks in the forest, we suddenly heard a lot of noise. A large group of men, wearing Russian military uniforms, was arriving. It was a group of about 40 men, some with medals and machine guns. We saw Combrig Martinov arrive, with his blonde, beautiful wife and two bodyguards, Wolodka Czurylow, and another man. There was also a Major, other officers, and some paratroopers among them. With them was a young Jewish man from Kletsk (Kleck), called Przepiurka.

Combrig Martinov made a very big impression on all of us. He was blond and handsome, of medium height, about 30 years old. When he looked at a person, he inspired respect and obedience. His military uniform was immaculate, and many medals were pinned on his shirt.

We didn't have enough food to feed all these people. At nightfall, Shlomo Olenski, Velvel Halperin, and a few of the Russians went into a village and brought back a cow. They killed the cow, and we cooked it and had a lovely, big meal. Not one part of the cow was wasted; we even used the intestines. Matel Finkelstein cleaned out the intestines, stuffed them with rubbed potatoes and fat, and cooked them like sausages.

The Combrig organized the partisans. Our group was named *Zuchov*. Lubka and I were chosen to cook for the military brigade. We all slept together in the same bunker, and I shared my blanket with little Luba Frank to protect her from the threat of rape. All the girls started to beautify themselves and flirt with the Russian men while Lubka Frank and I kept on working, day and night. We gathered wood, fetched water, peeled potatoes, cooked, washed, and mended the laundry.

All the young men were chosen to join the military: the three Olenski brothers, David, Abe, and Shlomo; Yossel Broida and his brother Itzik; Velvel Halperin, Szmul Kleinot, Haim Velvel Pribut, Moshe Rubinstein, Leibl Trus, Velvel Golda, Meir Wiszniewiez, Hershel the Drayster, Israel Brenner, and others. All the remaining men, women, and children – mostly girls – were organized into a family, under the supervision of Chaim Finkelstein. We felt safe and happy. We would sit around the fire and sing songs. Our happiness, however, was short-lived.

The farmer whose cow the men had taken followed their footprints, which led him to the forest. He informed the Germans in Bransk, who organized a battalion of local Nazis (W*lasowces*) – mostly Ukrainian – and sent them to the forest to attack our partisans.

On that particular morning, I woke up distressed after a restless night in which I had a terrible vision. I had dreamed of my mother; it was dark, and we were being attacked. In my dream, I saw the Russian Combrig's hat lying on the grass, and I ran and ran. When I woke up, I knew that we were in danger; that soon something like what I saw in my dream was going to happen. Yet, at the same time, I knew and believed that I would be saved; that I would be granted the same invisible, Divine protection and help as I had been granted in so many previous deadly situations. The sign was that I dreamed of my mother.

As I walked with little Lubka Frank on the way to the river to fetch water for cooking, I discussed my dream with her. We both agreed that it was already late in the afternoon; the Germans never attacked in the dark, so we were safe for that day, and we should not worry. We cooked dinner; everybody ate, and then laid down to rest. Lubka and I were getting ready to go to the river again to fetch water for tea. Just as we were about to leave, we saw Shlomo Olenski and Yossel Broida arrive. They told us that they were going to visit Mule Kleinot, who was wounded and was staying in Gittel Rubinstein's bunker. They asked us if we would like to join them. We said we would love to go, but first we had to ask the Combrig for permission.

The Combrig gave us permission to go with Shlomo Olenski and Yossel Broida. He also arranged for Hershel the Drayster to bring water from the river for tea. It took about 90 minutes to walk from the camp to the river. We went in the direction of Gittel Rubinstein's bunker, which was about half an hour away. It was a pleasant spring evening, warm and peaceful.

When we arrived at Gittel's bunker, we saw Mule Kleinot lying stretched out on the grass, his wounded leg bandaged, groaning with pain. We had just managed to ask him how he was feeling, when we heard the deafening noise of automatic weapons coming from the direction of our camp. We all ran. Even Mule forgot his pain; he stood up, grabbed a stick and ran with all of us.

We ran through an open landscape of trees, fields and farms. Early in the morning, we reached Chaim Kewlaker's bunker, where he was hiding with Little Stella Szcrecranska. The bunker was in the middle of a field. To me, it looked very unsafe. All around us, people were working in the fields. As we ran, they stopped working and looked at us. We stayed in Chaim's bunker for one day and one night, and then we left.

When we returned to the Bransk Forest, we first paid a visit to Gittel's bunker. We called her name, to make sure that she was still alive. Gittel told us that the Wlasowces were the ones who had attacked. They had surrounded the area near the river and were waiting for the partisans to come to fetch water. Hershel went to the river instead of Lubka and me. As he came closer, he saw the Wlasowces. He ran back to our camp. They followed him and attacked the camp with machine guns and grenades, taking our partisan group by surprise. A Russian man named Boris, and one Jewish man, Meier Wiszniewiez from Bransk, were killed. The others fired back with their machine guns and retreated to another location.

I realized that Lubka and I had been saved from death. If we had gone to the river, they certainly would have killed us. When the Russians returned, I heard them telling tales of the battle. I heard the Combrig telling his friends that he had lost his military hat while running through a field, just like I saw in my dream. I knew that I had been saved from death by Divine help.

I believe that when things are the darkest, God's presence is the nearest. God will help us if we seek Him in our hearts, but we should try to be worthy of His help. We should not hate others but be peaceful and truthful. We should not be jealous of others. We should keep the Ten Commandments.

MISSIONS WITH THE RUSSIAN PARTISANS

We all returned to the Bransk Forest. The Combrig began to organize the partisans. He sent groups of men on missions almost daily, to obtain food and to blow up railroad tracks. He also gave an order to simultaneously explode three bridges in three separate towns and sent three groups of partisans to carry out his order. Two of the groups left earlier, because they had some distance to travel. Our group was assigned to blow up the Bransk Bridge.

Another group of partisans, comprising Russians and Jews, was sent to retaliate against informers and murderers. They shot Frank Dniester from Zwirydy for informing the Germans about the bunker where Bobehe Rubinstein and the others were killed. They also shot a man called Koszak, who was a forest administrator. He would take in Jews and promise to hide them, but instead he robbed and killed them.

Paul Rasin read a death sentence in front of Koszak's family and told Koszak's children not to follow in their father's corrupt footsteps. They also looked for Adamczyk, who had informed the Germans about the bunker where Waska Wierszynin was killed, but they could not find him. He had run away; his house was empty.

The Combrig was obsessed with finding spies sent by the Germans to penetrate our ranks. Since the news of the war was that the Russian Army was advancing, the White Russian farmers around the Bransk Forest tried to find favor with the partisans by helping us with food and information.

A Russian man came to one of the farmers and asked the whereabouts of the partisans. The farmer gave him food and sent his son to inform the partisans about the inquiry. The Combrig arrested the man and questioned him. A handsome, quiet young man, who was new in our group, was afraid that perhaps the partisans would suspect him of also being a spy. One morning when he stood on guard, his rifle accidentally discharged. He panicked and shot himself. I saw him lying on the ground with a head wound. I was so distressed and upset that my heart went out to him. The Russian doctor looked after him.

An older, Russian man was found wandering alone in the forest. The partisans brought him to the Combrig for questioning. The Combrig was suspicious of the man and wanted to sentence him for spying, but Aloshka, the Russian who was in my bunker when we were attacked, vouched for the man and promised not to let him out of his sight. So the Combrig left the man in Aloshka's care.

We received marching orders. The Combrig selected a group, including Lubka Frank and me, to go to a different forest. We left the camp and traveled to a forest near Ciechanowiec, my hometown. When I said goodbye to my Jewish friends, they were sad and even jealous. They told Lubka and me that we were very lucky to be chosen by the partisans.

When we arrived in the other forest, we met a group of Russian partisans with machine guns. One man was different from the others. He was hugely overweight and had a beard. His name was Ivan Ivanovitch. A Communist Party Kommissar, he was very serious and bossy.

One morning, the partisans brought some leaflets containing German propaganda. They read the leaflets and laughed at them. Ivan Ivanovitch told them that it was forbidden to read German propaganda, that they would be prosecuted for this, and that the old rules were still binding. Combrig Martinov complained to us privately, not to Ivan Ivanovitch. He said that when the war was over, if people like Ivan Ivanovitch ruled so strictly, and if there was no freedom of speech, he was not sure if the Revolution had been worth all the suffering and sacrifices.

The Combrig also told his partisans to treat Jews with more consideration. He said they should not blame all the Jews when they had a complaint, but they should blame the person responsible by name, because all people are not the same. The Combrig's Jewish friend, Przepiurka, was a very brave man. He completed many successful missions. He also made sure that any raping of women or girls was punishable by death. The Combrig told me that the partisan group near Bielsk Podlaski had a typewriter. He asked me if I knew how to type. I told him that I had worked in an office in 1941, but only for a few months, and I didn't have much experience. Just the same, he picked me to go to the other group in the Bielsk Forest, together with three Ukrainian men.

One of these men was Zahar, who had been with us for a long time. The second was Fyodor, who had escaped from a prison camp and knew how to walk using the stars for guidance. The third man was Shevchenko, he was young and handsome and was dressed in the uniform of a German army officer. He had recently come to join the partisans, bringing machine guns and ammunition with him.

The Combrig did not completely trust these Ukrainians. He was testing them by sending me with them. He thought that if they really were honest and trustworthy, if they brought me alive to the Bielsk Forest, and if they treated me – a Jewish girl – well, then they could be considered to be acceptable. He sent us on ahead on our own and said that the rest of the group would arrive later.

The four of us left the camp. During the day we hid in the forests. We walked only at night, with a compass to guide us through many villages. When we saw a night watchman, Shevchenko told us to stop and hide. He would go to the watchman alone, pretending to be checking him, and ask for directions. In the evenings, we would go to the nearest local farmhouse to ask for food. All my companions were very good to me.

One Sunday afternoon, we arrived at the house of the village Soltys. The Soltys was hiding, but his wife came out and gave us food and vodka. My companions all drank and became very happy. They lost all sense of danger or fear and had no intention of leaving the house. The wife was very tense and frightened. She told me that at any minute she expected a visit from the Germans, who came every Sunday afternoon for dinner.

I walked in and out of the house, looking and watching, I kept warning my companions, but it was of no use. I felt trapped and helpless, so I started asking God for help. Finally, the men listened to me and agreed to leave the house. We were walking in the middle of the road, when we heard a car approaching. All of us jumped into a ditch at the side of the road and watched the car go past. It was full of Germans and drove straight to the house of the Soltys. I thanked God for saving us.

We kept on walking for many nights until we arrived at an isolated house where a contact man lived. The partisans knocked at his window. They said a password and the man came out of the house and began walking away without a word. We followed him through a field, then through a forest, and another forest, which was very muddy. We kept walking until, at last, we met up with a group of partisans.

There were many Russians, including about ten girls, in the group. As soon as we arrived, a very tall girl named Sonia came over to me with a soldier who carried a rifle on his shoulder. The three of us separated from the group and walked to a hidden bunker where the typewriter was kept. We typed inside the bunker, while the soldier kept watch outside. We typed the latest news from the front; the Russian Army was advancing, and they would soon be coming to free us from the Germans. The partisans handed out these news leaflets to the village people, who became very friendly. It was close to the end of the war, and they were afraid they would be punished, because some of them had helped the Germans rob and murder both Jews and Russians.

Every night, the Combrig sent different groups of people on various missions; one group was sent to blow up railroad tracks, another to obtain food. Only one person in each of these groups knew where they were going. The others just followed his lead. I asked the Russian girls if they wanted me to help them with the cooking, but they refused my offer. I asked the Combrig to send me with the partisans who were carrying the food parcels, and he gave me a handgun to use. There often were shootouts with the Germans, who would wait at the edge of the forest for us to come out of the forest on our way to the villages.

We carried food parcels all night until dawn. When we arrived back at camp, we would put all the food we had brought in a tent. We would be exhausted and would fall asleep instantly. When we woke up and wanted to eat, all the good food like eggs, bacon, or honey would be gone, and we would be left only with bread.

The Russian girls took the best food for themselves and their friends. Woloda Czurylow and all the Russian men who had come from the Bransk Forest were very cross at the girls' behavior. They complained that they were not used to such treatment. They told the girls that in the Bransk Forest, when Lubka and I did the cooking, all the food was always divided equally.

An acquaintance of our Combrig came to our camp from a nearby village. He was very excited. He brought the message that a taxi full of Germans was waiting at the edge of the forest. A few partisans with machine guns, Combrig Martinov, and the radio operator, all left with the messenger. I was puzzled. I wondered what would happen next. It didn't take very long until the partisans returned with a group of Germans in uniform.

The Germans told us that they were a group of *Volksdeutschen* who worked for the German police in Bielsk. They had been in contact with the Major for a long time. The radio was broadcasting that the front was getting closer and that the Russian Army would soon arrive in the area. They decided to come and join the partisans and said the war was nearly over.

That evening, while we were on our way to a village for food, the Russians told me not to panic if I saw Germans in the village. They told me that these Germans are our friends, and that they will come in a taxi to our forest. We arrived at the village to find all the farmers in a panic. They told us to run away because Germans were there. We asked them to tell us where the Germans were, and we would go and fight them. The farmers ran away in fright from their homes, leaving everything open. We went inside, opened the cupboards, and took the food. We packed it up and headed back to the forest.

When we arrived back in the forest, we met a group of about 30 Ukrainian *Wlasowces*. They had guns and ammunition and wanted to join the partisans. The Combrig divided everyone into groups and then he, his bodyguards, and all the partisans who had good weapons, left the forest. I was assigned to cook for a group of ten partisans with guns, along with the 30 who had recently joined us without their weapons. I was upset by the assignment at first, but after a while I felt happier because all of the men in the group were friendly and nice. We needed food, and the partisans found a way to obtain it.

The farmers from the villages hid their cattle and livestock from the Germans in the forest. One partisan, who was in command, made a deal with the farmers. He gave them receipts stating that they had helped the partisans, and in return, they gave us food. I cooked the food; it kept me busy and happy.

One morning, the Combrig and his two bodyguards came to our group and ordered me to come with them. He told the man in command of the group that he was sending me back, alone, to the Bransk Forest, with instructions. I was worried. I thought, *How can I go so far, 30 kilometers, to the Bransk Forest, alone, when I have no sense of direction?* When our group went out of the forest on a mission, I never looked around; I just followed the others.

There were still Germans all around the area and the White Russian villages were very unfriendly. But I didn't say anything. I got myself ready to go, and I left with the Combrig and his men. We walked until we saw a few houses in the distance. The Combrig sent his two bodyguards to collect food from these farmhouses, and he and I sat on a hill to wait for their return. The Combrig questioned me about the Jewish boy, Przepiurka. He had seen him talking to me in the Bransk Forest. He was anxious to know if Przepiurka had told me about his prior adventures. I answered that he never talked about anything important; he just joked about silly things.

I told the Combrig about my lucky escapes in the Bransk Forest, how we had been attacked by the Germans, how my best friend, Washka Wierszynin, had been killed, and how I escaped only with burned hair. In the meantime, the two bodyguards returned. I saw an amazed look on their faces when they saw that I was still with the Combrig. I stood up and walked on with them.

I was sad and troubled. I didn't know what would happen to me. I was so relieved when we finally arrived at the camp of the elite partisan group in a forest, where the Combrig's wife, Tasia, was staying. I hadn't even had time to look around, when Tasia came over to me with some fabric. She showed me one of the Combrig's old shirts as a sample and asked me to sew up a military blouse for her, the same style as her husband's. I was so grateful and happy that I didn't have to walk back to the Bransk Forest by myself, that I did my best to make a good blouse.

I cut the material and did all the sewing by hand. I was so absorbed with my sewing, that I forgot all my troubles and problems. I devoted all my attention to the blouse, and I succeeded. The blouse came out perfectly. It had two pockets on top and Tasia used a wide belt at the waist. When Tasia put on the blouse, she looked so pretty that everyone, including the Combrig, admired her. Of course, they praised the blouse. In payment for my work, Tasia gave me a pair of soft leather boots since my old ones were worn out.

We heard heavy bombardments and the pounding of artillery shells. Suddenly, we saw a whole division of Russian soldiers arriving in the forest. They all wore Russian Army uniforms, but they arrived distressed and empty-handed, without guns or ammunition and without any food.

The Combrig asked the Russians what had happened to their arms. They answered that they had loaded all their guns, ammunition, and food on a horse-drawn wagon and were walking beside it when a German machine-gunner, hidden in the forest, started shooting at them. Many of the Russian soldiers were killed. The rest of them ran until they arrived at our camp.

We had mixed feelings about the situation; we were happy that we had finally lived to see our saviors, the Russian Army, but we were not sure what was going to happen next. Were we really free, or were the Germans still in command? Everybody was sad and uncertain. The Combrig sent a few partisans to investigate the situation. The next day, they returned with the good news that the rumors were true. We were free, the Germans had left, and we were truly free at last!

We had prepared a lot of food in case the battle on the front line lasted a long time. Now, the partisans gave some away to the farmers who had come to the forest with their families. Everyone was excited and very happy; they shouted and drank. The partisans were very generous to the locals and gave them food and clothing. They gave them everything they had, shouting, "We are free, free!"

I stood alone; I was in no hurry to celebrate. Something was missing and I felt only sadness and emptiness. I had nowhere to go and no one to meet. I knew that for me, the war did not end just because the shooting was over. Still, I yearned to be able to forget. I had a longing to have somebody close to me to love, and I hoped that one day I would once again have a normal, happy life.

MORE SPARKS OF HOPE

It was August 1944. The Germans retreated and the Russian Army liberated us. The front line moved further away, toward Warsaw and we finally left the forest. It was a beautiful, sunny day. After living for so many years in the forest, under the shade of the trees, my eyes were not used to the bright sunshine, and I had to squint to keep from looking at the brilliant light.

All of God's creation had come back to life. The trees were covered with light green leaves, and the meadows were fragrant from the fresh grass and the small yellow flowers that were blooming above the grass. Everywhere, one could hear singing, from the partisans and from the birds in the trees. I heard the buzzing of insects and the croaking of frogs in the river.

It was a joyous occasion, and yet, all my sentiments, all my excitement about the beauty of nature disappeared, when I thought about all my relatives and friends who didn't have the privilege, the advantage, of living to see this day of freedom and beauty. It was a bittersweet moment that became increasingly bitter.

I walked with the partisans to a grand manor that had once been owned by a Polish lord. There were tall trees on both sides of the drive. The mansion was surrounded with gardens filled with colorful flowers and the view was beautiful. Inside, there were about 20 rooms and a very big kitchen. A qualified Russian cook did the cooking; his helper was a Russian girl. During the German occupation, the two of them had worked for the Bielsk police, but now they cooked for the partisans.

One morning, men from the Russian High Command arrived and asked to see the Combrig. They told him that all our partisans were required to come with them to the front line to fight the Germans. The Combrig showed them documents stating that he and his men only answered to a special department in Moscow. He said that if the Army needed help, he would lend them 30 men, but these men must be allowed to return to the rest of the group. The men left in two trucks and went to the front line. Later, they returned, with 100 German prisoners.

There were a dozen smaller houses on the land around the mansion. The *Upolnomoczenny* [Plenipotentiary] and a few Combrigs lived in one of these houses. They asked me to cook for them; they didn't trust the Russian cooks, because they had worked for the Germans. I would go to the farmers to collect food. They gave me eggs, potatoes, cabbage and all sorts of other vegetables and I cooked the food outside, just as I did when I cooked for the partisans in the forest.

One day, when I was busy cooking, I suddenly heard knocking and shouting coming from the direction of one of the smaller houses. I went closer and looked into the window of the house. I saw two middle-aged men. A younger man had told me that they were his uncles. Their names were Mitko and Zelko, and they were millers from the village of Bocki.

The millers had been in the Bielsk Forest with the Russian partisans. When the Germans attacked the partisans, they ran away to their nephew's hiding place. They had been hiding together for the past few months. Now, after they had survived, when they were happy to be free, the Russians wanted to arrest them for desertion and were threatening to shoot them. The young man asked me to intervene on his behalf, because he was innocent. He said he had never been a member of the partisans and would never have deserted them if he had been. I listened to his story and my heart ached. I felt that if Jews had miraculously been saved from death, this fact did not justify their being judged as criminals.

I finished cooking the meal for the officers, but when I served the food, I didn't look at them or talk to them. I was very upset. The officers saw that something was wrong and the Upolnomoczenny asked me why I was so upset. I told them that they were wrong to arrest and judge Jews for hiding in a Polish farm. I knew what kind of danger they had been in, running and hiding from death. They promised that the three Jewish men would not be shot, but that they would have to go to the front and fight. I went to the window of the small house and told the men what would happen.

The Combrig ordered a group of Russian partisans, including me, to take some prisoners to the headquarters at the front line, near the town of Hajnowka. We had to walk through the middle of a battlefield. The Germans were on one side of the forest and the Russians on the other side, shooting at each other. German planes were shooting at us from the sky. Every time we heard gunfire, we had to drop to the ground. The Combrig's two bodyguards, Woloda Czurylow and another man, came with us.

When the Combrig and his bodyguards first arrived at our camp in the Bransk Forest, I didn't like the bodyguard Woloda. He was very arrogant and sure of himself, laughing at anything and anybody. He was very handsome, tall and blond, and had a beautiful singing voice. I used to sit there, looking and listening, but I never spoke to him. When we arrived in the Bielsk Forest, Woloda told everybody how honest I had been in giving out the food and that I was not like the Russian girls, who were cheats. Slowly, I started to like him. I saw the better side of Wolodka, though I never thought of him as anything more than a friend. He was so good-looking that he could have had any girl that he liked.

When we walked through the battle at the front, I didn't know what to do; I just stood there. Wolodka came and grabbed me, he covered me to protect me from the bullets. I was so happy that I forgot all about the fighting. I wasn't frightened any more. I knew then that I must be in love with Wolodka, or that, at the very least, I had a crush on him.

We came to a village near Hajnowka where the Russian Army headquarters were located. The Combrig and the rest of the partisans arrived soon after. The Combrig read out orders to us and we all received documents stating that we were partisans and had to hand in our guns. He also read out the names of the members of our group in the Bransk Forest, Zukowski *otriad,* who had been awarded medals. Out of all the Jewish partisans, he called only two names: Luba Wrobel and Yossel Broida. We were told that we had to go to Minsk to collect our partisan medals from the headquarters there.

In the meantime, everyone was ordered to go to his or her place of birth. I had to go to Ciechanowiec. I was given a lift in an army truck that was traveling through the front line, in the direction of Bransk. When I arrived in Bransk, I met all of my Jewish friends from the Bransk Forest. I stayed at the house where some of the Jews from the forest were living. Many of the houses in Bransk had originally belonged to Jews but during the German occupation, Polish families had taken possession of all of them. Now, when the Jewish survivors of the war returned to Bransk, the Poles felt hostility towards them, because they were afraid that the Jews would reclaim their homes. Once again, we were disappointed by human nature.

One room of our house was occupied by a Russian army doctor. Soldiers would bring the wounded from the front line to him for emergency operations. It was a terrible scene. I shivered at the sight of the wounded soldiers, who were bleeding and moaning. I was shocked by the tragedy of war.

Although we were freed from the Germans, we were still very traumatized. We could not absorb all that was happening. We could hear the sound of mortars and automatic weapons being fired, so close by, that we were terrified. When we heard the sound of battle, we felt the same sense of danger we had felt in the forest, and we ran to the fields in panic.

One morning, we were standing in front of the house, when we saw groups of people without guns and without military uniforms walking toward the front line. We noticed that three Jews were walking with one of these groups. I stayed in the house with my Jewish friends for a few more days. The front line moved forward, and the Russians left Bransk. I did not feel safe living in Bransk with the Poles, who were not happy that the survivors had returned.

One day, Paul Rasin, from the Zukowski *otriad,* arrived in Bransk. He told me to go to the partisan headquarters in Minsk to collect my medal. I had not thought that the medal was so important, but it was an excuse to leave Bransk. I hitchhiked rides with army trucks until I arrived in Minsk.

The partisan headquarters were in a village called Peraya Loshitsa, which was near Minsk. When I arrived, hundreds of partisans were there from all over Europe – from Poland, Hungary, Yugoslavia, Czechoslovakia and other countries – and had already been waiting in confusion and disappointment to receive their medals for days. There was a big kitchen where we were given coupons. In exchange for these coupons, we received some watery soup and a piece of bread. We were all so hungry that all we could think about was food.

The same older Russian partisan who had managed to provide food for the partisans in the Bielsk Forest also tried to find food in Minsk. He called for me and another partisan girl, Ninka Vorobiowa, to come with him to dig out potatoes for dinner. We took baskets to a small field of potatoes and started digging. We already had dug out quite a lot of potatoes when we heard a scream. We looked up and saw a skinny woman with a long, sharp knife screaming at us to drop the potatoes. If not, she said, she would kill us with that knife. She swore that she meant it. She was the private owner of that small potato field. We dropped everything and ran for our lives.

Our lodgings were in a big barn. The owner of the barn worked as a guard at a *kolkhoz* [government cooperative vegetable farm]. He told us that if we touched or stole potatoes from the government farm, he would shoot us. He carried a gun and had orders to shoot dead anyone who stole even one potato or vegetable from that farm. I heard some of the partisans talking between themselves. They said that they would ask to be sent again to fight as partisans in enemy territory, because they couldn't stand the hunger any longer.

Ninka Vorobiowa was also consigned to General Kaposta's Soediniena partisans, but she was from a different otriad than mine. Ninka had a beautiful face and a charming smile. She was short and a little plumpish, but she was very friendly, clever and good-natured. Ninka was a godsend to my lonely soul. I felt happy and at peace when she was with me. From the time we met, we were inseparable friends.

Ninka told me that she was born in a small, White Russian village near the town of Kosowo, in the Brest oblast. Her father was a blacksmith and had a small farm. She had a younger sister and an older brother who joined the partisans. He and his group used to come from the forest to visit the family but somebody from the village informed the Germans of his visits, and they came to arrest him. The family's house was on a hill, so they saw the Germans coming. They left all their belongings and ran to the forest, where they joined the partisans. The family survived, but at the end of the war, the Army sent Ninka's only brother to the front line, where he was killed. Ninka told me that when she and her family returned to their village, they found that the neighbors, even her father's brothers and sisters, were hostile towards them. They had taken all of the family's belongings and were reluctant to give the stolen property back.

Ninka and I were very hungry, so we decided to go to Minsk and knock on people's doors to ask for bread. We found that the city was in ruins. Some people were living in ruined, half-destroyed buildings. Much of the rubble had not been cleared and we walked through debris of stones and broken bricks.

In an empty square in the middle of the city, we saw a few hundred German prisoners under the guard of Russian soldiers. We asked for bread, but the answer was that they could not spare any, because the coupons they received were issued for such a small piece of bread that it was not enough to share. We were so hungry, we decided not to wait any longer for the medals but to return to Poland. Before we left Minsk, we wanted to say goodbye to Wolodka (Czurylow). We asked if anybody knew where he was and finally found out where his group was staying.

Ninka and I walked and walked for hours until we reached the army barracks. There were only a few guards. Wolodka and the others were away, working in an airplane factory. The factory was a long way from the barracks; it was underground, and they did not let civilians inside, so we had to leave without seeing him. I thought that this must be destiny and that Wolodka was not meant for me. I was grateful to have realized that despite all the drama and trouble I had been through, I was still capable of love. I knew that one day I would find true love and make a new life for myself.

I told Ninka that it would be a good idea if we went to the RAIFO (the Russian taxation office) in Minsk to ask for a letter of introduction, because in 1940 I had worked in the RAIFO in my town. Such a letter could help us obtain work in Poland. We received a letter of introduction for both of us, with instructions to go to Brest.

The journey from Minsk to Brest, and then to Kosowo, took more than four weeks. The trains didn't travel on a regular schedule;

would stop suddenly in the middle of a field for hours or days, and nobody knew when they would start again. When that happened, all the passengers would get out of the train, make a fire in the field, and cook tea or soup. When we saw the train starting to move, we spilled our soup and ran to catch the train. This happened many times on the journey.

Finally, we arrived at Ninka's parents' home, in a small village a few kilometers from Kosowo. Ninka's father and mother welcomed me like a daughter. They were very fine people, who had suffered many of the same ordeals as the Jews. The mother was still mourning the loss of her beloved son. Some of the village people who had robbed the family were angry that they had survived and returned to reclaim what belonged to them.

It was the summer of 1944, and the sun was shining. I took a walk across a field. I could smell the sweet aroma of grain. In the evening, Ninka took me to meet the girls from the village. It was sad to see so many teenaged girls sitting on the lawn and singing love songs, without even one young man being present. I asked Nina where the young men were. She told me that some of them had run away with the Germans; the rest had been mobilized into the Russian Army. The girls were ordered to work in forced labor.

Ninka's parents were glad that Ninka was going with me to work in an office. We said goodbye to Ninka's parents and sister, and her father took us in his wagon to Kosowo. From there, we caught a train to Brest. When we arrived at the RAIFO office, we showed them the letter from the head office in Minsk. They asked us if we would like to go to work in a small town called Dibyn (in Belarus), near Kobryn. We, of course, were unfamiliar with the town but agreed to go. All we were thinking about was that we would have food. We thought that in a smaller town, there would be a better chance to buy food from the farmers. We were given a letter of introduction to the office in Dibyn and we left.

We took a train from Brest to Kobryn. A Jewish man was working at the train station. He asked us if we were Jewish and took us to his house, where he lived with his mother and two sisters. They had also survived with the partisans in the forest. The man's mother and sisters had some sewing that needed to be done. They had some fabric they wanted us to make into new dresses. A Polish woman, who lived in the other half of the house, also needed some sewing done. We stayed with them for a few weeks to do their sewing, and in exchange, they gave us food.

One market day, we caught a lift to Dibyn with a farmer. Dibyn was a little village surrounded by forests. In the autumn, when it rained, the roads would flood, and nobody could get in or out of the village. All the people in Dibyn wore clothing that they had made themselves. The men wore linen trousers with a string at the waist, long white shirts and slippers. The women all wore scarves on their heads and very long, gathered skirts.

There was no RAIFO office in Dibyn. We had nowhere to live and slept in a farmer's barn. The people told us that all the young men of the village were hiding in the forest and that they had organized a group to fight against the Russians. At night they would come back to the village to collect food. During the war, the village had cooperated with the Germans. Now, all the villagers were worried that they would be arrested. The owner of the barn told me that it was a very dangerous place for a young Jewish girl to live in, because during the German occupation, the men of the village had robbed and killed a lot of Jews. I decided that Dibyn was not the place for us to stay and we should move on.

When we were in Brest, we had been told that the punishment for leaving work without permission was punishable by five years in prison. I decided to risk it; I picked up my knapsack and left. Ninka was frightened about being sent to prison, but she decided to come with me anyway. We walked until we reached Kobryn and then we caught a train to Brest, where we went back to the RAIFO office. We were very frightened. We thought that we would be punished for leaving Dibyn but, to our surprise, the Director did not punish us.

He forgave us and didn't report us to the authorities. Instead, he sent us somewhere else, to a town named Malaryta, east of Brest.

We traveled to Malaryta on a train that passed through the town and began to work in the RAIFO office, which was located in a large wooden house with many rooms. We had nowhere to live, so for a few weeks we lived in one of the rooms in the office. I noticed that a short, shabbily dressed, pimply-faced man in his thirties was a frequent visitor in our office. I never paid attention to him, but Ninka, who was very polite to everybody, always talked to him and smiled at him. She had the most enchanting smile.

Baranov, the Director of our office, told us that this shabby little man was a very influential boss. He was the real ruler of the district, including Malaryta and the surrounding villages. Officially, his position was subordinate to that of the Soltys, but he was the (Communist) Party man who watched over everything. He was feared even by the Soltys himself. I was romantic at heart. I had to like a man in order to be able to spend time with him, but Ninka was a realist. She knew that if she wanted to have a future in the New Order, she needed help and protection. There was a Russian saying: *Blat wishey Narkoma*, which means 'Protection is above the law.'

One day Ninka told me that we were going to move out of the office to a private room. We moved into a beautiful room, in the home of a very nice White Russian family. We ate our meals in a government restaurant, but a meal there consisted only of watery cabbage and a small piece of bread.

We were earning very good money. However, the food sold on the private black market was very expensive. One kilogram of butter could cost an entire month's wages. We were given coupons for a month's supply of food, at cheaper government prices. The coupons were exchangeable for one bottle of oil, one kilogram of fish, and some bread. We were so hungry that we ate all the food that was supposed to last us an entire month, in one day. One of the girls who worked with us frequently went to visit her family, who owned a farm in a village named Zamshany (in Belarus). When we went there with her on Sundays, we were given a very good dinner.

Our landlady was a very nice woman. She and her husband were in their fifties. They were very sad. The woman always kept a Bible and prayed to God for the safety of her two sons, who had been taken into the Russian Army and sent to the war. Her only consolation was her pregnant daughter-in-law, who was staying with them. She used to show us the photo of her tall, handsome sons. The daughter-in-law was short and not pretty, yet they treated her like a jewel. They did not know if their sons would ever return, and the expected baby might be the only connection to their son that they would have left. The landlady often gave us a plate of soup without charge, and we appreciated this very much.

A White Russian girl from Malaryta worked in the office next door to ours. She was tall, very well dressed, and snobbish. When I was not around, this girl had a heart-to-heart talk with Ninka. She said that she wondered why Ninka chose to be such a good friend to a Jewish girl. She said that personally she hated all the Jews.

The girl told Ninka that when the Germans took over Malaryta, they shot all the Jews of the town, about 5,000 men, women and children. They buried their victims in a mass grave, in a pit they had prepared in the field at the end of town. One wounded man escaped from the mass grave. The girl had found him hiding in her shed. She called the Gestapo and they shot him. The Gestapo rewarded her, giving her a lot of beautiful dresses and clothing that had belonged to the murdered Jews. They also gave her a job in the Gestapo office, where she worked until the Russians came. Ninka listened to the girl's story and later told it to her boyfriend, the Party boss. One morning, that girl disappeared, and we didn't see her in the office anymore.

The Director of our RAIFO office, Mr. Baranov, was a tall, grayish man in his late fifties. He wore spectacles and always had an amusing expression on his face. He was always polite, whereas his wife was always rude. She was short, energetic, very talkative and always complaining. She was the Director of the Malaryta food warehouse. A Jewish woman from Brest had once been sent to check up on her work and she hated all Jews since then.

There was a lot of hatred in the villages around Malaryta. People who did not have many possessions were jealous of others who had stolen a lot of clothing, bedding, and furniture from the murdered Jews. These jealous people would bring lists of the names and addresses of the robbers to our Director, Mr. Baranov. The lists even included descriptions of the stolen property.

Baranov called me into his office. He gave me a list of the stolen items and the addresses of the robbers. He ordered me to go to those villages, collect the goods, and bring everything to him. The next morning, I went to look for a ride with the farmers who came into town. Near the hospital, I found a farmer who gave me a ride to the right village. I went to the government office in the village and showed them Baranov's letter. They sent a Russian official with me to collect the stolen items, according to the list.

When we confronted the women at the houses on the list, they saw that I was Jewish and looked at me with great fear in their eyes. They could not understand how we had specifically picked them to return stolen goods. They thought that I had come back from the dead to claim these things. Their consciences were heavy, and they began to tremble. They ran to the next room and brought out parcels, urging us to take them.

I was puzzled and bewildered. I did not know what to expect, but the Russian official was very self-confident, even aggressive. He ordered a horse and wagon and requested the owners to put all the parcels of used blankets, clothing, shoes and eiderdowns into the wagon. He then ordered them to give us some food. The farmers always wanted to be on the best terms with Russian officials, so they gave us sausages, bacon, and eggs to eat, as well as some vodka.

Instead of being thankful for the food, the Russian official became jealous of the farmers. He said to me, "Look, I was a soldier. I was wounded. My wife and children are always hungry, and these farmers have so much food." The Russian official decided to organize a kolkhoz, a Soviet type of communal farm, for the whole village, even though he didn't have orders to do so. He knew that none of the farmers were interested in a kolkhoz, but he also knew that they would be afraid to refuse or protest. He was very proud of himself, saying, "And then they will have food rations, like me."

The official and I brought all the clothing that we collected and gave it to Baranov. I saw him put everything in the big garage behind the office. When I signed the document for the clothing, I saw that it stated that if the goods were not distributed according to the law, the person responsible for the goods would be sentenced to ten years in prison.

I looked through the office window and saw that Baranov was giving out clothing and blankets from the garage to certain officials, in exchange for special favors. I did not care what he did with these things, but I wanted a receipt from him stating that I gave him all of the stolen items, as required by the document. Baranov plainly refused to give me a receipt. I pleaded with him, I told him that I would be sent to jail, but he laughed and promised to bring me food in jail.

I knew that I was in trouble. I understood that without a receipt from Baranov stating that he had received the items referred to in the document as 'government property' in good condition, I could be jailed for irresponsibility. I had witnessed what happened to other people in similar situations. People disappeared and others were put in jail without trial for even the smallest of transgressions. There was a local joke in Malaryta: "We have three kinds of people – those who are in jail, those who have been in jail, and those who will go to jail."

In the house next door, there lived a Russian man, a former partisan. He was married to a local girl and held the position of

Director of Food and Animal Skins. A farmer gave this Director a sheep in exchange for a little salt, because no salt was available in our district and as the Director was cooking the sheep, the aroma drifted out all over the yard. It smelled wonderful. All of the neighbors were standing around and whispering.

The next thing we saw was the Director being arrested by the police. As Director of Food, he had been giving extra food to people, even if they didn't have coupons. That is why he was arrested. A new Director took over after that. He gave out food only in exchange for coupons, and there were no exceptions.

The Director of Horses and Vehicles told me that the previous Director of Food used to give him extra food parcels, in exchange for horses and vehicles to collect the monthly food rations for the whole district from Brest. Now, he refused to provide the new Director of Food with vehicles. If the allocated food was not collected on time, then another district would take it. Thus, our district was left without a grain of salt, no sugar, and no kerosene.

I was restless. One night, I had another dream. I dreamed that I was walking on a bridge and wished to go all the way across, but then I saw my mother, telling me to turn back. The next day, I was walking with Ninka to the market when two young women stopped me and asked me if I was Jewish. They wondered why I was still in Malaryta. The women were Jewish, two sisters who had been born in the town, but they didn't want to live there anymore, and had moved to Kovel. They advised me to come to Kovel. They said that a lot of Jews were making their way from Kovel to Poland, then to Romania, and then to Mandate of Palestine. The sisters were flour merchants. They showed me a house in Malaryta that belonged to one of their customers. The woman frequently came to them in Kovel to buy flour, and her husband worked for the railway. They said that this couple would help me go to Kovel.

When I arrived home, I remembered that I had left my boots to be repaired in Brest. Baranov was going to Brest, and I asked him to pick up my boots for me, even if the repair was unfinished. He did bring my boots to me, but they were not repaired. Although the boots had been in the shoe repair cooperative for many weeks, the repairs would never be done without a bribe.

A new law was instated: all Polish citizens were required to go back to Poland and all the White Russians from Poland were ordered to settle around Brest. In Malaryta, a Commission was set up to send all the Polish citizens back to Poland. Baranov was a member of the Commission. I had my partisan papers, showing that I was born in Ciechanowiec in Bialystok Province. I asked Baranov if I could go back to Poland, but he said that he would see to it that I was not allowed to go to Poland, because he needed me in his office.

Baranov was short of workers. Most of the men had been forced to join the Russian Army. I knew that I would have to leave without informing him. Ninka had been sent away on a three-month study course and I was very lonely. Baranov gave me a document that was valid for two weeks, entitling me to go with a list to another village to collect more "government property."

I saw that this would be the perfect opportunity to run away to Kovel. I told my landlady about my plan and asked her not to tell anyone where I had gone. If Baranov was to inquire where I went, she was to say that she thought that I had gone to the village as he had instructed.

At the back of the house where I lived, there was a field of potatoes. Workers were digging them up and there were many bags of potatoes in the field. The landlady asked me to go to the Director and ask him for a few bags of potatoes. He agreed to give them to me, but in exchange he wanted me to help him get his horse from the man who stole it from him during the war.

First, we took the potatoes to my landlady. The Director filled her cellar with potatoes; she paid him a few rubles and she was very, very happy. It was impossible to buy any potatoes privately. That same night, I packed my bag. I said goodbye and left in the darkness. A guard stopped me and asked to see my documents and where I was going. I showed him Baranov's paper and told him that I was leaving on official business. He let me go.

I arrived at the house of the woman recommended by the Jewish sisters. We waited until midnight and then went to the station to catch the train. The woman's husband, the railway worker, opened a train car for us. Inside the car, there were German women, children and older men. All of them were on their way to Siberia.

When we arrived in Kovel, we left the station and went straight to the home of the sisters from Malaryta. The house was very busy, full of many different types of people. I saw two men who had just recently arrived from Russia. They had originally come from Warsaw and already had documents that would enable them to cross the border into Poland.

I met another young girl there, who was born in Malaryta. She was an officer in the Russian Army and had fought near Berlin. She had been wounded. Now, she was going to Poland and from there, to Mandate of Palestine, where her brother lived. She had paid for a Polish document. She advised me to go to the Commission and ask for a document allowing me to cross into Poland, too. I went to the Commission and showed them my partisan papers. I told them that I wanted to go back to Bialystok. They wouldn't give me a permit because I didn't have a release paper from my job, so I returned to the sisters' house empty-handed.

A group was leaving for the border that night. They advised me to come with them and promised to smuggle me over the border in their train compartment. They entered the train, and I hid outside nearby. I saw Russian soldiers entering the compartments to check the passengers' documents. When they turned on their flashlights, rays of light fell near my hiding place. I crawled under the train to escape, even though I knew that I was in mortal danger. If the train moved, I would be killed. While I was under the train, I heard somebody calling, telling me that it was safe to come into the compartment. The checking was finished. I climbed up onto the train, and I knew, somehow, that I was safe.

We passed through a town called Chelm. After that, we arrived in Lublin. There, I stayed with the group, including the girl officer from Malaryta. She had parcels of clothing with her, and every day I went with her to the market to help her sell the clothing. We spent the money from the sales on food. When we ran out of things to sell, the group moved on to Romania, on their way to Mandate of Palestine. I didn't have the money to cover the expenses of that trip, so I was left behind in Lublin, alone. I decided to go back to Bialystok. I hoped that maybe I would be able to find a relation or friend and was able to board a military train on its way there.

BIALYSTOK

It was dark outside. At a station near Bialystok, a woman with parcels entered the train and took a seat on the steps of the passenger car. When we arrived in the Bialystok station, the woman, who thought that I was a smuggler like herself, said that she would take me through the back streets, so that the Russians would not catch us and take away our goods. I didn't say anything, I just followed her.

We were ordered to halt. Two uniformed Polish policemen asked to see our documents. I showed them my partisan papers. They screamed "Jew!" in my face and did not return my papers. The woman started to cry and plead with the police. She said that she did not know that I was Jewish and that she herself wasn't Jewish. Both of us told the police that the woman didn't know me, that she had just met me on the train and so they let her go.

The policemen said that they would shoot me. When I heard the click of their guns, I threw my bag, which contained everything I owned at the policemen, and ran away as fast as I could. I passed a few houses; my instinct told me to run into a yard and hide there. I found a narrow space between a toilet and a fence. I stood there, very frightened, and didn't make a sound. Inside the house, someone switched on a light. They were looking for me.

I stayed in that yard until morning. Then I walked down the street, asking people where the Jewish community was located. They told me that it was on Mlinowa Street. I went there and asked the caretaker of the building here I could meet some Jews. He advised me to go to the market, where all of the Jews went to shop. There, I met Lubka Frank from my partisan group. We were both very happy to see each other again. Lubka told me that some of my relations from Sokoly were living in Bialystok, not very far from where we were standing.

Lubka took me to an apartment on the first floor of a building at 1 Piekna Street. There I found the brothers of my Auntie Sorche and Auntie Lea, Avraham (Avramel) and Chaim Goldberg. With them was Faigele Tabak, their niece, who had survived the war under the protection of Mrs. Piekutowska in the village of Lendowo-Budy.

I was so very happy to see them alive that I was filled with joy to the depths of my soul. After thinking that I had lost everyone, it was just wonderful to discover a few members of my extended family had survived. We were about to exchange stories of our ordeals when, in a brief moment of silence, they suddenly asked "Where is your luggage? Don't you have any belongings?" I told them about my encounter with the Polish police and my lucky escape at the cost of losing all I owned. They agreed that I was indeed very lucky to be alive. They told me that only the night before, the same night I escaped from the police, 15-year-old Yaakov Litwak, a young survivor from Sokoly, had been innocently walking home in the dark from the Bialystok train station when he was shot and killed by the Polish police.

I asked them how they found our mutual relative, little Faigele in Lendowo Budy, and they told me all that had happened until the time we were reunited. Moshe Janczeman, a survivor from Bransk, told Avramel Goldberg that he had heard that a little Jewish girl named Faigele Tabak, was in Lendowo-Budy. Avramel walked there with his friend, Moshe Lev, to see if the rumor was true. As they walked through the forest near Lendowo-Budy they saw a little shepherdess, whom they recognized as Faigele. Avremel talked to Faigele in Yiddish, saying, "Faigele, don't you recognize me? I am your Uncle Avramel who used to bring you chocolates and lollies from Warsaw."

Instead of answering Avramel, Faigele ran away screaming, "Save me! The Jews are chasing me!" She ran into the house where she was living with an old Polish lady and hid under the bed. Avramel talked to the old lady of the house, but she did not intend to let the girl go. Avramel went back to Bialystok where he was working as a carpenter. He waited until he finished renovating his apartment. His brother Chaim and a partner had a blacksmith business. Avramel was determined to get his niece back to her family so, when they had saved up some money, they hired a Russian soldier who had a truck to drive them back to Lendowo to collect Faigele.

On the way to Lendowo-Budy, the Goldberg brothers stopped at a house in Sokoly. In that house were ten Jewish survivors who were planning to have a reunion party that night. Two of the men, Benjamin Raclaw and Benjamin Gorkowitz, offered to go with Avramel to collect Faigele. They hired a military vehicle and came armed, as they knew that their efforts to get their niece back would not be met with a peaceful response. The old lady had grown extremely fond of Faigele and they would have to rescue her. Under cover of arms, the two brothers entered the home in Lendowo-Budy and retrieved their niece, the only surviving member of her immediate family.

On their way back to Bialystok with Faigele, the men returned to the house in Sokoly. In the house, they found the results of a massacre.

Members of the Polish AK, who had freely murdered both Jews and Russians in the forests during the German occupation, came that night, February 17, 1945, to Sokoly. The AK broke into the house, and with their machine guns they murdered seven of the Jewish survivors from the death camps and forests. Only one man, Avraham Kalifowitz, survived. He had hidden under a bed and was covered by another man's dead body. He saw the bandits pull the boots and clothing off their victims' bodies, but in their haste, they did not see him.

Those murdered on February 17, 1945, were:

- David Zholty, 33 years old, who had survived the war thanks to some good Polish people who saved him, only to be murdered by Polish bandits at the war's end.
- Shamai Litvak, 19 years old.
- Shamai's brother, Shaike Litvak, 13 years old. The Litvak brothers also survived the war thanks to good Polish people. Now, they were dead.
- David Koschewsky, 28 years old. He had survived the concentration camps in Majdanek and Auschwitz, only to meet his death at the hands of a gang of murdering Poles.
- Batya Weinstein, 20 years old, from the town of Swiczienin. She had also survived the death camps and was engaged to marry Benjamin Raclaw.
- Sheina Olshak, 22 years old, who survived the war hiding in the forest. Sheina met her untimely death inside a Polish town.
- Tolka Olshak, Sheina's beautiful four-year-old niece. Only a few weeks earlier, Sheina had taken her niece back from a Polish woman who had sheltered her during the war. Now, Tolka was tragically killed by beastly murderers.

THE FATE OF MY FAMILY

My future husband Chaim Goldberg, who I knew from my days in the Sokoly ghetto, told me how he had survived the war together with his older brother Avramel Goldberg. The two brothers managed to survive in the forest for a little while as they were strong and armed, both being members of the resistance in the ghetto. They made their way to the home of a farmer they knew from before the war, and despite many complications, and the need to pay "rent" the farmer helped them.

Chaim and Avramel, together with their cousin, Moshe Maik, Moshe's father, Michael, and another young man from Sokoly, Monik Roseman, had hidden together on the farm of a Polish farmer named Kalinowski. The farm was near the village of Bruszewo, not far from Sokoly. The farmer helped them build an underground bunker, whose entrance was cleverly hidden underneath a toilet near the barn. Although he demanded payment for doing so, there is no doubt that this farmer risked his own life and that of his family to save a handful of Jews.

Moshe Maik, my husband's cousin, was the son of Michel Maik who in turn was Chaim's sister's son who died in Sokoly before the war. She had three children. One, her daughter Lea, married and went to live in Israel before the war but her two sons Israel and Michael remained in Sokoly. Israel Maik married Dina and had two children in Sokoly.

Michal Maik was a highly educated man who taught Hebrew and English to children. A matchmaker introduced him to a wealthy family from Vilna who had two daughters. One daughter was tall and good looking, the other one was short and very skinny. Michal preferred the taller one as his bride as the other daughter was so small that he thought that she was still a child. The parents discussed a dowry and set a date for the wedding. At the *chuppah* [bridal canopy] the bride's face was covered with a lace veil and she wore a crown on her head. Michal stood happy under the chuppah. He gave the bride the ring and they were married. Later, when they uncovered the *Kalah's* [bride] face, he saw that there was a mistake and he had been tricked. He had married the wrong sister, but it was too late. His father took the money for the dowry and told him to keep quiet. Michal brought his new wife to Sokoly and told his friends that the matchmaker had cheated him by giving him the wrong sister. But the truth was that she was a very fine woman. Her name was Cipa, she was good natured and pretty and charming. She sang like an opera star.

Michal and Cipa had one son named Moshe who was tall like his father and good looking like his mother. He also had his mother's good nature and musical talent. When Moshe heard a song, he could go to the piano and, without a music sheet, play the song like a professional musician. Moshe was also a member of the Jewish resistance and a radio mechanic. Before the war, he used to repair Kalinowski's radio. Moshe was such an honest, good, and likeable person, that Kalinowski promised to help him if a day ever came when Moshe was in trouble and his life was in danger.

Avramel, Chaim's older brother, was the best carpenter in Sokoly. Before the war, Avramel worked for Kalinowski. The Goldberg brothers' father, Israel, was a blacksmith who had also done a lot of work on the Kalinowski farm with his youngest son, Chaim. Chaim was a member of a Zionist youth movement and a member of the Jewish resistance in the ghetto in Sokoly.

The three boys amassed some weapons and ran to the forest where they were eventually hidden by Kalinowski after paying a large sum of money and handing over material goods to him. From the bunker that they built themselves underneath an outdoor toilet on Kalinowski's farm, they carried out daring resistance missions. On one such mission they set fire to Sokoly, deliberately burning down most of the Jewish homes there. They did this so that the Poles would not get the benefit of acquiring murdered Jews' homes.

To this day, our family is still in touch with Kalinowski's family, and we do what we can to help them by sending them packages and gifts. Unfortunately, Michal was separated from his wife Cipa before going into hiding and was unable to save her. Avremel was also married with a child and separated from his family when he went into hiding. The two wives and the child were murdered in the Holocaust.

Chaim's father, Israel Goldberg, stepmother and the rest of his siblings and their families were all murdered in the Holocaust.

Chaim's Uncle Tevie, his wife Rachel and three daughters Raszka, Malka, Sara, and two sons Elimelech and David Eliezer were also murdered in the Holocaust alongside their families. Two daughters, Adasa and Lea managed to survive because they married and left for Israel before the war.

Two sisters and two brothers from Ciechanowiec, members of the Ptasliek family, had survived the war hidden in a bunker by a righteous, gentile farmer. Before we left Bialystok, they told me what had happened to all the Jews from Ciechanowiec, including my family-

In 1942, the Germans ordered all the Jews to assemble in the marketplace. From there they marched them to prearranged mass graves and shot them all.

When the Ciechanowiec ghetto was still in existence, my brother, Avraham Moshe Wrobel, worked outside the ghetto in a water-driven flourmill owned by a Polish miller, Mr. Malyski. Avraham Moshe was tall and strong, and Mr. Malyski liked him. My brother used to smuggle flour and grain into the ghetto and all the Jews blessed him for this. When the ghetto was liquidated, Malyski kept the boy hidden for a few months until he was forced to leave his hiding place. Avraham Moshe was killed by Polish bandits.

My mother Golda (Tabak), my stepfather Chaim Kawka, and their little son Shmuel hid in a bunker inside the ghetto, together with some of their relations. When the Germans discovered the bunker, they shot and killed all of those hiding there.

I understood that I had come back to Bialystok by God's providence. It was my wish to get away as far as possible from Poland and never to return to that cursed land of hatred and antisemitism. I had suffered so much, only to return there against my will. But when I found Chaim, Avramel, and Faigele alive and well, I understood God's reason for bringing me there. I knew that from then on, I would never be alone again. I remembered Chaim Goldberg, whose two sisters were married to my uncles, from our days in Sokoly ghetto when I used to borrow books from him. He was a kind, honest man, with a shy smile. As soon as I saw him again, I understood that he was my perfect match.

For some time, I did the housework and shopped in the market. I liked the way Chaim gave me money to do the shopping, but never asked me to account for every penny.

Chaim Goldberg and I were married in Bialystok in May 1945. The guests at our wedding were all of the survivors from the Bransk Forest, from my hometown Ciechanowiec, and from Sokoly, my husband's hometown.

In May 1945, the war was not yet over, but in Bialystok it was more or less peaceful, except for the hatred shown to the Jews by our supposed protectors, the Polish police. Not so long ago, they had been murdering Jews and Russians in the forests. Now, they killed them in the city, in the dark of night, whenever they had the chance.

We lived in Bialystok, on the first floor of a building, above a restaurant. We occupied half of the upstairs apartment; the other half was occupied by my husband's partner, David Sprzonsko, and his wife and son. Every evening, as soon as it became dark, we would shut and lock all the doors and windows in the apartment, for fear of bandits.

One evening, looking through the window, we saw a tall, blond, young man shouting from the street, "*Partisanka*, open the door." We presumed that the young man was a Polish bandit, and were reluctant to open the door. But he was persistent. Eventually, when he identified himself as one of the Bocki Jews who had been arrested by the partisans in the Bielsk Forest, we did open the door. The young man had come to thank me for defending him, for talking on his behalf to the Russian Combrig and for saving his life.

The Chairman of the Bialystok Jewish Reconstruction Committee, Dr. Shimon Datner, organized a theater on Polna Street, where a group of actors, who were all survivors of the concentration camps, performed musical dramas. On Sunday afternoons, all the survivors gathered there to see the show. It is impossible to describe the feelings, the overwhelming emotions, that these plays awakened in all of us. They reminded us of the biggest traumas we had experienced.

Each of us, including myself, felt such emotions especially when Dora Rubina, a skinny little woman whose hair had not yet fully grown back since she had been in the concentration camp, performed and sang. Dora Rubina sang many different songs and each one touched the survivors' hearts.

When Dora Rubina performed, singing about a mother who had left her child, she was transformed into the real mother, suffering that terrible loss. During the performance, we heard hysterical cries in the theater, from women who were again reliving their pain. I was so absorbed in the performance that I forgot where I was. I was heartbroken.

I remembered my Uncle Pesach's little son Hershele, who had told us in distress, with the voice of an adult, of the pain and humiliation he had suffered when he was separated from his mother in 1943. He was left alone in a Polish village. The Polish children took out his penis and pulled at it because he was circumcised. They called him "Jew" with venom in their voices and laughed at him. From the time of that painful separation, even after he and his mother were reunited, he had been afraid to sleep, lest his mother would leave him again.

When Dora Rubina performed songs about the people who were packed into the trains on the way to Treblinka or Auschwitz, there were people in the audience who relived the parting from their families. I also felt the truth in her song about shadows. The emotions expressed were exactly how I had felt when I wandered alone in the dark.

The following are translations of some of the Yiddish songs sung and performed by Dora Rubina in May of 1945, in Bialystok:

The Last Night

A black night, a terrible night

The rain is dripping loudly

A solemn procession walks

Women, children and old men

Now they are packing them into boxcars

Like canned fish, so tight and full

They all know very well where they are going from there

And as the train moves a bit, the wheels start to turn

The rhythm knocks in tune

"To death, to death, we go, we go."

And in the boxcar it is darker

Than in the street at night

We hear the barking dogs

Someone, like a devil, laughs

And playing in the people's hearts

Are tragedies, deeper than the sea

And people begging

"Have pity, give me the poison pill, help me."

And mothers cuddling their children

For the last time

Kissing them and kissing them

Without end, without stopping

I am there with my mother

I kiss her and I know for sure

That as soon as the train stops

The last hope will disappear

And suddenly, I have a thought

"NO! I will not finish up like this!"

I feel my mother's tears on me

My young blood boils

My death will be another

With a push I open up the window

Away from the wheels and noise

I jump out of the boxcar

And when I stand up from my fall

The train, I hear, is far away

But in my ears still rings

My mother's voice; she calls to me.

Around me is the dark of night

"Oh, what shall I do?"

I sit and think

And I wipe from my face

The blood from a wound

And my mother's tears.

Now We are Like Shadows

Now we are like shadows

Who wander late at night

In a life without light

You don't know what to await

Strange is your fate

Every door, every shutter

Is closed to us today

You are driven by need

No one asks how you feel

If a heart in you beats

For we are like shadows

That the night spreads around

Only she understands where everyone went

Who to life, who to his end

These shadows will soon disappear

From the darkness of the night

Figures will appear

They will shine very bright.

In a Remote Lithuanian Village

In a remote Lithuanian village

In a little house afar

Through a window not so big

Seeing children in the street

Boys and girls, blond and fair

And together also there

Looked out, so sad, apart

A little boy, so nice and dark

His mother brought him there at night

She wrapped him up, kissed him and cried

"Here my child you have to stay

Listen to what I have to say

I have to hide you here tonight

Because in danger is your life.

With the children you should play

Quite obedient you should stay

No Jewish word, no Jewish song

From today, just go along

The child cried, "No, no!

Please don't leave me here alone"

In her arms she took him

And softly sang to him

And as soon as he slept

She left him all alone.

It's cold in the street with a blowing wind

A voice is heard,

"*Oy, mine kind* [my child]

I left you all alone, in strangers' hands

Because to save your life I meant"

In the street it's dark, it's cold and late

A mother walked, she cried and prayed

"O God, have pity on my child!"

To Moses' mother she is compared

For like Moses on the riverbank

In danger, lonely in the wind

She left alone her only *kind*.

IN SEARCH OF A FUTURE

Under the Potsdam Agreement, Lower Silesia was given to Poland. Before the war, these territories belonged to Germany. Jews who had survived the war in Russia and were arriving back in Poland in transports, found temporary shelter in camps that were set up in Lower Silesia. Along with the Jews coming from Russia, survivors from the concentration camps, bunkers and forests also made their way to these temporary camps.

Moshe Maik and Chaim's brother, Avramel, traveled to Waldenburg (Walbrzych). After a few weeks, they returned to Bialystok. They told us to immediately pack our possessions; we were all going to Waldenburg. We left behind all the bedding, furniture and other heavy possessions. Chaim and I, Faigele, Avramel, Moshe Maik, his father Michael, and Michael's new wife, Esther, went together to catch the train to Waldenburg. The train was very crowded with Polish people. We had to make the journey sitting on the roof of the train.

When we finally arrived in Waldenburg, Avramel and Moshe took us to a house that had formerly belonged to a Nazi who absconded after the war. In the house, there was everything that we needed: heating, beds, blankets and lovely furniture. Avramel and Moshe took over an empty shop on one of the main streets, where they set up a radio and electrical appliance repair business.

Moshe was a radio mechanic and the others worked under him. Faigele went to the local school. Esther and I looked after the house and did the cooking. Every day, I traveled by train to take home-cooked meals to the men in the shop.

One day, on my way to the shop, I looked on in amazement at a group of Polish soldiers who were hitting and shouting at a group of older Germans for not working properly. Upon seeing this scene, I felt that life is so very complicated; nobody should take anything for granted.

On April 25, 1946, my first child, my beautiful daughter, was born in Waldenburg. We named her Goldie, after my mother, who was murdered in Ciechanowiec by the Germans in 1942.

During the period that we lived in Waldenburg, hundreds of thousands of Polish people arrived there. Among them were many members of the AK and antisemites. Chaim and I decided that Waldenburg was not the right place for us to build a future for ourselves and our young family. We understood that we, and all the Jewish survivors, needed to live in our own land, Mandate of Palestine, the land of the Bible, the land that was promised by God to the Jewish people; today, the Land of Israel.

I had a happy surprise: my relation from Sokoly, Dina Krasnoborski, was alive and well, and came to visit us in Waldenburg. She had survived the war in the German concentration camp at Bergen-Belsen and was living in a kibbutz, a Zionist collective community, in a village near Waldenburg, with her husband, Chaim Sarna, a man from Bialystok who had survived the war at Theresienstadt. Dina told me that the whole kibbutz was ready to travel to Mandate of Palestine. She said that we could come with them, because she would register us as relatives and we agreed. We took only one rucksack with a few of our belongings, and the baby's diapers.

We put our baby daughter in a special, long cushion. We also took Faigele, who was ten years old. We were ready to travel wherever the group would take us. We left the beautiful house with the lovely furniture, in search of a peaceful, happy future. We traveled to Steinhagen in closed trucks. There, amongst German refugees, we received our documents and boarded a train. At last, we arrived in Berlin.

Germany was divided into four zones occupied by the Allied forces. From Berlin, we traveled on another train through the Russian Zone to Hanover, which was in the British Zone. We stayed in Hanover for a few days. From there, we traveled through the French Zone until we arrived in the American Zone, at Schlachtensee. We stayed in Schlachtensee for a few weeks. We were then sent to a Displaced Persons [DP] camp called Herzog, near Hessisch-Lichtenau, not very far from Kassel. A few more of these camps, such as Goldkop, Eshwaige were nearby.

The Herzog DP Camp housed a few hundred families. We were looked after by UNRWA (United Nations Relief and Works Association), and the Joint Distribution Committee (the Joint), which provided us with clothing and food. We shared one room with another family – Josef Citrin, his wife, and their baby. My husband's brother, Avramel Goldberg, and his wife Tauba, a survivor of Auschwitz, also reached our camp from a refugee camp in Austria.

One day, we received a letter from America, from my mother's relatives, the Tabak family. They wrote that they had sent us a parcel of blankets and ten packages of food from CARE International. They also sent us papers to fill out, to apply for a permit to go to America.

I overheard my husband and his brother, Avramel, discussing whether we should go to America or to Australia, instead of the Land of Israel if we could not gain entry there. They said that Australia was the best choice. They had two aunts and their families who were already living there. Australia, they said, is far away. It is the fifth continent of the world, and it is common knowledge that no wars have been fought there. They said that Australia is the best place to escape hatred, poverty, and war. Their final argument was, "Australia is a country made up of immigrants and people from all over the world, just like us. There, we will find peace and happiness."

In the meantime, Avramel found some of his friends who were preparing to travel illegally to Palestine by ship, because the British, who were ruling the country under the Mandate, would not allow any new Jewish immigrants into the country. Avramel took his wife Tauba and Faigele, and they left for Mandate of Palestine. We were not allowed to join them because of our baby.

We wrote to Chaim's aunts in Australia, and they sent us an immigration permit application to complete. We soon received a letter telling us to go to Frankfurt to be approved for a visa. The visa was approved. Then we were told that we would have to wait in the DP camp until our permits and visa were sent to us, and until a ship traveling to Australia was available.

We were restless. I felt a terrible longing to see ten-year-old Faigele who had been taken away from us by my husband's brother Avramel to Cyprus. We asked and inquired everywhere if there was any way that we could go to Palestine. We received a letter from Avramel and Faigele from Cyprus urging us to join them.

Another group in the camp was organizing an illegal way to get to Palestine. They were planning to travel through to Italy through the Austrian Alps to leave for Mandate of Palestine with the *Bricha* – a group of young Zionist leaders who were helping Jews to get to Palestine. There were 150 people in the group, most of whom were old men, young children, and pregnant women. We decided to travel with them.

We gave a letter to our neighbor, Josef Citrin, so that he could claim the ten CARE packages from America. We left with the group. We were told that it would be best if we didn't have any luggage to carry, because it was going to be a very long, difficult journey. I kept my boots on even though they were heavy. They were brand new leather boots, the most valuable thing that I owned.

On a very dark night, we started to climb the highest mountains between Germany and Austria. It was a treacherous journey. The Austrian Alps were very high and steep. I was pregnant again, and my boots were heavy and stiff. I was so tired that I wasn't sure I would make it across the mountains. It was dark and slippery. We walked in single file, one behind the other. The boys from the *Bricha,* who were our guides, worked very hard. They caught everyone who slipped, pushed everyone who was stuck, and helped carry the children.

Our year-old daughter, Goldie, was very heavy for her age. Because we were so close to the border, we had to be very quiet. My husband carried Goldie in his arms all night long because she wouldn't let anybody else carry her. She only wanted her Daddy. If someone else tried to carry her, she would scream. In the morning, we arrived at a kibbutz in Austria. There, Chaim fell ill. He had a very high fever. The doctor gave him tablets but for two weeks the fever did not break. The doctor almost gave up. Then God helped us and Chaim recovered.

We then had to travel from Austria to Italy through the mountains. The hike was a little bit easier than it had been from Germany to Austria. When we arrived in Italy, we were arrested by the Italian Army, but they let us go after a day. We were sent to a transit camp in Milano. At first, we stayed at Via Uniona 5, and then at a place called Scola Kadorna.

Chaim was still weak from his illness. He developed an infection in his finger. A nurse in the camp treated him by cutting the infected finger open with a pair of scissors. After that, the pain was unbearable and he ran high fever again. It turned out that the infected finger was gangrenous. Chaim was sent to a hospital in Milano, where the doctors successfully operated on his finger. After that, the fever left him, and he soon recovered.

On December 1, 1947, I gave birth to my son, Jack, in Milano Hospital. From Milano, they sent us to the Fermo DP camp, which was located in a large, warehouse-like building divided into small rooms with canvas walls and doors. Each family was given one room. The canvas walls were about two meters high. Two hundred families lived in this building under the same roof. In the quiet of the night, we could hear intimate conversations between couples, because there was not enough privacy. There was a communal kitchen. We were given soup and bread each day, but we had to buy additional food. The little bit of money that we had was spent on food.

The Bricha told us that only single men and women were now being sent from Italy to Mandate of Palestine, because, at that time, the British troops were being withdrawn from the region. The Arabs in Mandate of Palestine and the surrounding countries were attacking the Jews. Soldiers were needed for the War of Independence, which followed closely on David Ben-Gurion's declaration in May 1948, of the establishment of a Jewish State called Israel.

I felt that because of Chaim's poor health, he would not survive the many hardships and hunger associated with war. I thought that perhaps for that reason, we should reverse our plans and go to Australia instead of Israel. My husband's two aunts Haya and Rachel had emigrated with their families to Australia before the war. I sent a letter to the Hebrew Immigrant Aid Society (HIAS) in Frankfurt, asking them to forward the permits and visas for Australia to us in Rome.

Next door to us lived a man named Lewin, with his wife, daughter, and son-in-law. His son-in-law worked at the Joint Distribution Committee. One evening, Mr. Lewin came to our room and told us that a woman from Rome who worked at the Joint had come to the camp, looking for people who had papers to travel overseas. He knew that we had such papers and wondered why we didn't report to her.

My husband didn't say anything. I told Mr. Lewin that we had recently received papers from Rome, but we thought it was a refusal. We had sent three papers to Rome and received the same three papers back, but with no visa. Mr. Lewin asked to see the papers. He looked at them and then he told us that the little stamp printed on the reverse side of the permits was the visa. He said that he wished this had happened to him and thought we were very lucky.

The next morning, we went to the office of the JOINT at the camp and were told to go straight to their office in Rome. There, we were told to move to the nearby Cinicitta DP Camp, which housed many Jews and Yugoslavians. There was a movie studio close to the camp. We saw Gina Lollobrigida, the Italian movie star, and her husband, who was the camp's doctor.

We received a letter to call the office of JOINT in Rome. We traveled from Cinicitta back to Rome by train and passed many beautiful historical buildings on the way. My husband enjoyed all the wonderful sights of the city, but I had problems on my mind. I hadn't expected to travel so soon. I had already stopped breastfeeding my son, who was then nine months old. My daughter was in the camp, ill with measles, isolated in a room with the other sick children.

At the JOINT office, we were interviewed by Miss Elkes. She told us to go back to the camp in Cinicitta and pack our things, because we were to be sent to a camp in Bogliasco. After packing our luggage, we sent it to Bogliasco by train. That evening, when we arrived in Bogliasco, we went straight to the camp office to ask for a place to sleep. Instead of giving us a room, they told us to go immediately to Genova, to a ship.

In December 1948, I, Luba, my husband Chaim, our two-and-a-half-year-old daughter Goldie, and our one-year-old son Jack, boarded the ship MN Napoli in Genoa, Italy for Australia. It was an old ship that had recently been repainted and the red paint was still wet. My son Jack had started crawling at that time and as he did, smudged red paint all over his trousers. We had no luggage; our small number of belongings – food and clothing – were sent in the wrong direction to a camp in Kruglasco, Italy.

All the women with children had sleeping quarters in a very big cabin low down in the ship. The men had cabins higher up in the ship. We were among a few hundred people of different nationalities, mostly Italians. One night there was a very big storm. The ship shook and heaved, and the sailors ran up and down. The passengers all woke up in a panic, afraid the ship was going to overturn and sink. My daughter woke up screaming and did not stop until I took her upstairs to her father. The dining rooms at mealtimes were half empty because most of the people were seasick. The women cried that they were going to die and would not live to see their families in Australia.

Traveling with us from our camp in Cinicitta, Rome, were four families with children, and a lot of single men. Three of the families were together in the cabin deep in the ship but one family traveled first class. The lady used to visit us each morning to show off how nicely she was dressed. I couldn't have cared less, but one lady, a Mrs. Zuffora, was cross and jealous and the two women bickered a lot. Mrs. Zuffora called the other one, *Sctaplerka,* but it did not stop her from calling to visit again the next morning.

I did not expect to travel so soon; it was a miracle that the children survived the trip because they were very sick with fevers. We adults were given macaroni and red meat. There was no special food for the babies, but luckily, one of the waiters gave me some milk for them.

Two young men in our group could speak a bit of Italian and the ship doctor gave the children penicillin injections, but only when we paid.

The first port of call was Port Said. Many small boats carrying Egyptian merchants surrounded our shop and advertised their merchandise. My husband bought a very nice photo album. The next port was Ceylon, now known as Sri Lanka. A lot of men from our ship took a boat and went to visit the port town. They came back excited, saying that they had traveled on rickshaws and had a lot of fun.

The first stop in Australia was Fremantle; we were all excited to have reached our dreamland. Australian officials boarded our ship to check our documents and asked us to fill out papers as to what jewelry and money we had brought to Australia. People were scared to reveal what had brought because in Europe the officials used to take away whatever you had. In Europe you could be caught and arrested for smuggling if you had any valuables. Of course, we had nothing, so we were not concerned.

A few citizens from Fremantle also boarded the ship and asked if there were any tailors among the passengers. Tailors in Australia were called Professors because there was a shortage of tailors. The next port where we stopped was Adelaide and a lot of passengers went to town to shop. The whole journey from Italy to Melbourne, Australia took five weeks and in January 1949, we finally arrived at our destination.

PART II

OUR ARRIVAL IN AUSTRALIA
MEETING OUR AUSTRALIAN RELATIVES

As the ship docked, all the passengers ran to the deck to look for familiar faces. We were all very excited and happy. People shouted when they recognized a familiar face. All around me I could hear happy sounds in a variety of languages. The atmosphere was exciting and joyful. Waiting for us were a lot of my husband's relatives: his two aunties, Rachel and Haja, and many other cousins.

Auntie Haja was a skinny little woman with straight gray hair, who dressed simply but neatly. She had been a shopkeeper all her life and she trained her five boys to help her in the shop back in Poland. Haja's husband, Zalman Lew, was a very active man and when he saw that his wife and five sons could manage the shop without him, he became restless and wanted to emigrate. He had come to Australia in the 1920s and as soon as he settled, sent permits to his family so they could join him. But Haja refused until Zalman Lew sent permits for Rachel and her children. They were happy to go straight away. Auntie Haja had wanted to wait longer in Poland but decided she had better leave everything and go quickly to Australia before her sister, a widow, grabbed Zalman Lew.

In Melbourne, Australia, Auntie Haja opened a tobacco shop in Lygon Street, Carlton and they lived in the back of the back.

Zalman Lew had a horse and cart and sold clothing and other assorted items to farmers out in the country.

Auntie Rachel was from Lomza, a town in the Bialystok region, not too far from my hometown Ciechanowiec. She was already in her sixties when we arrived in Australia. After her first husband perished in the war, she remarried an older gentleman, who worked in Watkins's Butchery. Rachel had three children – Max, Libby and Toiba. Her younger daughter, Toiba, her husband, Moshe and two children, Aida and Issy, also lived with them. She was plump, had a slightly wrinkled face and gray hair thinly spread on her head. She walked a little heavily and her face had a sad expression and she never smiled. She dressed in long, loose clothing, but when she went out shopping, she put on her black coat and hat. To me she looked pretty. She had a small nose, blue eyes and a heart of gold.

There were a lot of single men from Rachel's town, Lomza, who had arrived in Australia in the 1920s and could not find work for the first few months. Rachel let them stay at her place sleeping on the lounge room sofa and she gave them a bowl of soup every day, all free of charge.

Auntie Rachel's house was a double-story terrace house with a front veranda and an iron fence with pointy iron tops. Inside the house was a long passage from the front door to the kitchen, covered with shiny linoleum. On the right was a sitting room with a floral velvet settee and two velvet chairs, then a dining room with a table, chairs and an old buffet, where the family, including my family, used to have dinner during the first three months until we were settled. The stairs led to the top of the house where the bedrooms were. In the kitchen there was a wooden ice chest and every morning a man delivered a big block of ice.

Auntie Rachel's older daughter, Libby was a good-natured woman who always had a smile on her face and looked happy. She was blonde, blue-eyed, plumpish, dressed simply and was always clean and neat. She was kept very busy helping new migrants who had language difficulties.

Her husband was the opposite. He was stern, seldom had a smile, was of medium height, clear complexion and handsome. He took pride in his looks and dress, but he was selfish. He came from the same city in Poland as Auntie Rachel and she had sent him a permit to come to Australia with the assurance that he would marry her younger daughter, Toiba, whom he knew very well as his sister's girlfriend.

When he arrived, he refused to marry Toiba. When he was threatened with deportation, he agreed to marry the other daughter, Libby. They had three beautiful boys, Aizik, Haimy, and Solly, but Libby was not very happy. Her husband refused to give her enough money for housekeeping although he earned plenty working as a farrier and used to buy himself five suits at a time.

Libby was always cleaning the house, yet it never looked clean because it needed painting and repairs. The sink in the kitchen was a wooden one. No matter how much she pleaded with her husband to renovate the kitchen, he refused. It didn't matter so very much to Libby then, until her sister, Toiba bought a house opposite Libby's and renovated it so that it looked like a palace. Then the dirty little kitchen really upset Libby. She found a job cleaning offices in the city from 6:00 a.m. until 10:00 a.m. and she started saving money for the renovation.

We were pleasantly surprised to discover that my best friend Luba Frank was in Melbourne. She had been my companion in the Bransk Forest and my partner in cooking for the partisan group. They called her the Little Lubka and me the Big Lubka. She did not look little anymore. She was tall and all grown up. She told me that she had an uncle in Sydney, and he had sent her a permit to come to Australia. She had already been to school in Sydney, and she could speak, read and write in English. She had sent permits to the Olenski Brothers, David, Abi, Solomon and Cousin Dina and she lived with them in a cottage in Station Street, North Carlton. Some mornings I took the children with me, and we went to visit my friends from the war years, the Olenskis, in their cottage in Station Street, North Carlton.

David Olenski had already found work as a laborer in Smorgon's meat processing factory in West Footscray and he arranged for my husband to work there with him. A special bus was sent at six o'clock every morning to pick up all the new migrant workers.

In the beginning we lived with Auntie Haja's son, Leibl Lew, his wife, Sara, and their 13-year-old son, Benny. Benny was disabled, his muscles didn't work, so he was completely dependent on his mother for everything: feeding, dressing and even using the toilet. He could not talk and was only able to make noises, but his mother understood him and devoted her life to looking after all his needs.

When we arrived at Auntie Sara's house in Amess Street, North Carlton, my daughter, Goldie, was two years old and my son, Jack, was one. On the ship Jack, my son, was still crawling, but in Melbourne Jack stood up and started to walk. Our happiness was clouded when we watched Auntie Sara's son for the first time. Nobody had warned us how helpless he was, lying on the carpet, unable to speak or make proper sounds.

We lived in Cousin Sara's house for about three months; January, February and March 1949. Each morning after my husband left for work Libby and I ate breakfast at Cousin Sara's place. I would then put the children in a big old pram that Auntie Rachel had given us and walk with Libby and the children to her place where we would collect sandwiches and a bottle of milk. From there we would go together to a park in Princes Hill with her youngest, four-year-old son, Solly. It was summer, the sun was shining, the children were happy playing. In the evenings, we went to Auntie Rachel's for dinner.

It was a very hot summer. In the evenings when my husband came home from work, we would put the children in the big pram and go for a stroll around the streets of North Carlton. One day the children were thirsty, so we went into a milk bar and asked in sign language for a bottle of lemonade and four glasses. The shopkeeper would not serve us but as we did not speak English, we were unsure as to why.

Perhaps because the trauma of the war years was still very much with us, we presumed that he was antisemitic and that was the reason for not serving us, as we had not argued about the price. We asked our relatives about it, and they explained that Australian people are really very nice and that the milk bar owner was not allowed to sell a bottle of lemonade in the shop by the glass and he could be punished with a fine.

My husband's dream was to be able to work in a knitting factory but although he knew how to work on a hand knitting machine, all knitting machines, in Australia were electric and all the jobs were taken. One lucky morning, when I was at the Olenski's home, sitting at a table were about half a dozen young men playing cards and talking. I listened to their conversation, and I heard one young man saying that he quit his job at the knitting mills in Rathdowne Street. He had bought machines and was starting a factory for himself. That evening, I told my husband there was a job vacancy in Rathdowne Street at B & G Knitting Mills.

In the early 1950s only a few people owned cars. A relative of ours, Beryl Kurlender, had come to Australia in the 1930s and had made a living as a door-to-door salesman. He had a wife, Ricka, and two children, Sheina and Alex. Beryl bought a big old car and traveled to the country to sell clothing to farmers. He was only in Melbourne on the weekends.

Beryl was very good-natured, and he tried to help us as much as he could, so when we told him about the prospect of a job for my husband, he took him in his car to the factory and they hired him. The award wages were a week, but because they had to teach him to use the electrical equipment, he received five pounds per week for the first few weeks. When he knew how to work properly on three electrical machines he received seven pounds per week, the same as the other workers. In the busy season when there was plenty of work, they gave him a lot of overtime and he received bonuses. Often, he earned 14 pounds weekly, and we were very happy to be able to save some money.

Our dream was to move out of Cousin Sara's house to any place we could call our own private home. As I walked with the children, I saw big garages behind people's houses. I told my husband that I would not mind living in such a garage as long as we could have our privacy. With two little babies even renting a room was impossible.

Again, we were lucky. Our friends, the Olenskis told us that they knew of a bluestone cottage that was in such bad condition that nobody would want to buy it. This cottage was situated at 220 Johnson Street, Fitzroy. I was ready to buy it without looking inside, but how could we buy it when nobody knew the owner?

We called on our relation, Beryl Kurlender again who took us to Johnson Street in his car. He knocked on the neighbor's door and asked who the owner was. The neighbor did not know know but told us that a woman came there to sleep late at night. Mr. Kurlender waited until this woman came and she gave us the owner's address in Northcote. Good Mr. Kurlender was not lazy, and it was already quite late at night when we arrived at the owner's house in Northcote. He opened the door in his pajamas, and we made an appointment to see this bluestone cottage.

When we went back the car would not start. Mr. Kurlender rang his partner who arrived in his car to tow us. He tied our car to his with a chain and drove away without looking back, all the way to the Kurlender's house in Princes Hill. Only then did he realize that our car was missing. He had lost us in the middle of the road. We waited for an hour for him to come back, and this time he did tie it properly, but it was nearly morning when we all arrived safely at our homes.

LIFE IN FITZROY, MELBOURNE

The owner of the little bluestone cottage at 22 Johnston Street in Fitzroy came to our assistance when we approached him about buying the house. Auntie Haja's youngest son, Robert Lew, was a returned soldier, an educated and good-natured man, and he arranged for his mother and Auntie Rachel to lend us money. We gave them promissory notes from the post office and signed to repay the loan on a three-monthly basis.

The owner asked for 650 pounds for the house but when we were in the corridor near the solicitor's office he arranged with Cousin Robert that we should give him 300 pounds in cash but put 350 pounds as the 'official' amount paid for the house on the contract, because under real estate regulations of the time, the vendor was not allowed to sell the house for more than the listed valuation.

We were delighted to move from Cousin Sara's house to our own home. The house was dirty, smelly and had damp walls, but we felt happy and excited to face the challenge and to renovate. Around the front of the cottage was an iron fence. Inside the front door was the main room and to the side were stairs to an attic. Down one step was the bedroom with a window opening onto a small garden. In the yard next to the garden was a small dark kitchen with a door to the yard, then another little room, then a bathroom with the pipes on the floor letting water run out on the yard. Half the yard was covered with a roof over a large table which was very handy in the summer when I did all the kitchen work on it.

In 1949-1950, it was very hard to find good tradesmen, but our cousin Robert Lew brought over two people who agreed to repair the house. They got rid of the garden and connected the kitchen to the bedroom. The roof leaked badly but they refused to do any more work and demanded to be paid the full amount. We wanted to be rid of them, so we asked Robert to pay them the full amount and they left. My husband knew something about working with iron because he had been a blacksmith in his father's business back in Poland before the war, so we started to repair the roof ourselves.

We tried to buy corrugated iron sheets, but it was very difficult to get building materials. Chandler's store told us to go to the town hall where we put our names on a long waiting list. Most building materials were only sold on the black market and only to builders whom the traders knew as there was a shortage of materials. My husband bought a big soldering iron and repaired the roof, so the rain did not come in anymore. The walls were broken, and no cement or plaster was available, so we dug to find lime in our backyard and used it to patch them.

We then covered the walls with beautiful floral wallpaper with little blue and pink flowers, and it looked beautiful. We bought a dining room table and chairs as well as a buffet from the auction rooms and we put new shiny linoleum on the floor. With a tablecloth and a bunch of plastic flowers, the front room looked lovely.

We rented out the room on the yard to a single man to help us pay off the debts. For 30 shillings a week I changed the linen for him and helped him with shopping. This man, Mosze Wajman, worked in Plitkin's Rubber Factory and was very good-natured. Every Friday he brought home a pay packet of 17 pounds worth of wages plus overtime, but I noticed that on Sundays he stayed in bed all day. When I asked him about it, he told me that every Saturday night he played cards and lost all his wages, but the people were so nice, they treated him like a king. He said the women were beautiful and gave him coffee and cake.

I lent him ten shillings to see him through the next week and I bought him a dozen eggs for two shillings, one pound of butter, a bottle of milk, a loaf of bread, some meat and soup every day for no charge. He did not like to accept charity, but I told him that because I did not have a fridge or ice chest, I could not keep soup anyway, so I was happy to give it to him. The next time he got his pay packet he gave me two pounds and began to do so every week.

Then one day he told me that he had to move out. He apologized because he knew that we had debts to pay. He said he really would have liked to stay but the couple he played cards with insisted that he move in with them. I told him not to worry and that I would get another boarder. A few weeks later, I met Mosze Wajman's new landlord. He stopped me and said, with kind of an accusation, "Take him back." He had believed Mosze was a well-to-do gentleman because he would arrive each Saturday dressed like a lord and lose 15 pounds at the card table without any complaint. The new landlord wanted to borrow a few hundred dollars from Mosze, but it had turned out that Mosze did not have a penny to his name and that his impressive appearance was due to his one and only suit.

It was lucky for Mosze that he had a father in America who sent him money for fares, so he went there to stay with him. I advertised the room, and the next day rented it out to a man, Jack Burstein, who was a shoemaker by trade. He worked all week in a shoe factory and worked in our yard making custom-made new shoes to order for private customers on the weekends. He talked and worked with a mouthful of nails without swallowing any and he was a very good shoemaker who made very beautiful shoes, although each pair took him a few weeks to finish.

I did my shopping nearly every day. I put Goldie and Jack in a big pram and went to Smith Street because it was close to our house, and it was the biggest shopping center. Everything was plentiful and very cheap. I bought food to last a whole week for one pound. I cooked soup every day; soup with vegetables and lamb shanks and rolled oats. Milk was delivered to our doorstep from dairy owners by horse and cart in bottles.

The children spent a few hours a day at a free local kindergarten, next to MacRobertson's chocolate factory. In the evenings, after my husband came home from work, I would go to our neighbor's house, and she would teach me how to use the overlock sewing machine. She was also a new migrant and took her children to the same kindergarten. Her husband worked in an underwear factory and used to bring home a lot of ladies' lingerie to overlock at nighttime and at weekends. They owned two overlockers – one had three rolls of cotton and a knife to cut the material. I learned how to sew on the overlocker, but I needed the lady's help when the cotton broke.

My friend's cottage was in better condition than ours, but ours was in Johnson Street and hers was at the back of a lane. Her next-door neighbors were not happy people. Their children were neglected, the house was dark and there was no linen on the beds. On Friday nights there was a lot of noise and broken windows.

When my children began to go to kindergarten, I was able to work for a few hours a day at the Melnik factory, a knitting finishing factory in Richardson Street, North Carlton. It was a long, single-fronted cottage and the factory used all the rooms.

The owners had a three-year-old girl, and the wife was pregnant again. They worked and lived on the premises. Their partner, together with his wife also worked on the machines. They had two children who went to school.

The two partners bought knitted fabric from a knitting factory. They cut the fabric with an electric cutting machine into different sizes. The two overlockers did the overlocking, a buttonhole machinist made the buttonholes, a button machine sewed on the buttons, a finisher did the finishing, a presser pressed them, and the completed cardigans were delivered back to the knitting factory who gave the partners a cheque.

Those people really struggled. The pregnant lady cleaned, cooked and worked on the machines and the partner couple also worked very hard. It was difficult for immigrants in a new country with no knowledge of the English language, with no pension from the government and no close relatives prepared to help. So, the only solution was hard work.

A lot of new immigrants saw what people could achieve in Australia in a few years with hard work and they tried to do the same. Yet these people who had survived hell before coming here were very happy; they looked to the future; they knew that Australia was a beautiful country where they could save up to buy a house and have a good future for their children.

One day when I came to work, I found there were some new people in the residence. It was the boss's brother and his wife and son who had arrived from overseas, and they all squeezed into the same little cottage. All day the new arrival watched his brother's hands as he repaired the machines, and it made the boss very nervous. His hands shook and he pushed the screwdriver into his hand instead of in the machine. They called on a very inexperienced doctor who gave him too many penicillin injections and he had a heart attack. He had to stay in bed and could not even go to the toilet. He recovered after a few weeks, but the hardship placed on the family was enormous.

Although my husband worked overtime, we still had a lot of free time to ourselves. We went for a picnic in Fitzroy Gardens every Sunday. We prepared sandwiches, cake, fruit, and blankets and put everything in a box. My husband made delicious coffee. He boiled water in the kettle, boiled milk, put in Nescafe and sugar and poured it in a big thermos. I took the children and the box in a very big old pram, and we marched along Smith Street to Fitzroy Gardens. On sunny days the gardens were full of people and children; it was full of people, activity and noise, with a very pleasant atmosphere. We went to Captain Cook's cottage where for a few shillings we saw the original cottage as it was when Captain Cook first came with his ship to Australia.

Despite the obstacles we faced, we increasingly liked Australia for the safety and freedom we experienced and for people's general acceptance of us. When we arrived in Melbourne in January of 1949, I was very frightened of the people. I thought that everybody was looking at us and wondering if we were Jewish. At that time, we did not speak or understand English. After a short while, I began to feel that Australia was the right place for us, where we could be happy and secure.

On Saturday nights, I went to visit the cousins in Drummond Street, Carlton, and we went to the cinema together. I used to take a bus from Johnston Street, Fitzroy. One evening as I waited at the bus stop, I was joined by a lot of people who came out of the pub. A few of them were very drunk and I felt scared. I was used to drunk people in Poland behaving really badly, especially young males, but to my surprise, these people behaved like real gentlemen. When the bus arrived and I held back from boarding it, I heard them shouting: "Move, make room – a lady is coming." And they let me go on the bus first.

We had arrived in Australia after much suffering and trauma. We found peace and happiness in this God-given country and decided to work hard, do the right thing by Australia and the people in there. Once, on our way to the cinema we found a handbag with 20 pounds in it near a bus stop; that was the equivalent of two weeks' worth of wages, but we handed in the bag together with the money to the police.

Another time I went to the Regent Cinema on Johnston Street. Robert Menzies had just been voted in again as Prime Minister and he appeared on the screen giving a speech. I heard a lot of people booing and protesting and I expected them to be punished or even arrested because there were police present, but nothing happened.

I remembered how in Stalin's time, when the Russians came to our town in 1939, there was a hairdresser who spoke up and said that he did not like the way that, no matter how long you waited in the queue in government shops, you could not buy anything, and that the only things available were on the black market for exorbitant prices. His business rival reported this to the authorities, and he was sent to Siberia. I felt really lucky to be living in a country where people were free to protest against a Prime Minister and not be punished for it.

MITCHELL STREET, BRUNSWICK, MELBOURNE

As soon as we paid off our debt to the Aunties, we decided to sell our bluestone cottage. The Menzies Government did not have strict controls on prices and competition was the Price Valuer; no more black market. We were able to buy everything we wanted from the shops.

We put our house for sale on the real estate market with an agent and we sold it very quickly. We started looking for a bigger house to buy and became aware that a vacant house cost double the price of an occupied one. We bought a vacant possession house in Mitchell Street, Brunswick at auction. We paid double the price that an occupied house would have fetched because we did not want to hurt people by hiring a lawyer to evict them. Others laughed at us, but we felt good for doing the right thing.

The house needed many repairs. We bought a load of concrete, but the concrete maker used so much sand that it melted in the first rainfall. We paid the seller the full price despite our troubles and marked it down to experience.

After a while, I became a very experienced overlocker. I then found a job in Little Bourke Street, in a factory that made knitted woolen sweaters. I worked only from nine in the morning to three in the afternoon, but I earned as much money as the workers who worked full-time, because I worked on a piece-work basis. I was the only overlocker in the factory, and I had to work at high-speed so as to get all the work done. My role was to overlock all the knitted jumpers, and if I did not finish the work during the week, I had to come in on Sundays to complete it.

After work, I had to rush to pick up the children from school on time. Once, I was late coming to collect Goldie and she was missing. I was frantic, I ran home and she was not there either. I ran up and down the street calling out and asking people if they had seen my daughter. Then, to my relief, an elderly woman came around the corner, walking with little Goldie who was crying and sniffling. The woman had taken pity on Goldie, because she was crying and could not find her way home. I thanked the lady and was very careful not to be late again to pick her up from school.

My son Jack was not old enough for school, so I paid Auntie Rachel to look after him. I used to bring him to Rachel early in the mornings before taking Goldie to school. Sometimes Rachel and her husband were still asleep, so I left Jack on the veranda and told him to wait till they opened the door. He said, "I will not cry. I know that you've got to pay off the house and also pay interest." I remember that our interest rate was at 40 percent; we wired the amount directly to the owner's account. This was in the 1950s.

We tried to spend as much family time together as possible during the holidays. Show Day was a very big holiday in Melbourne; all the shops and factories would close. When Goldie was five and Jack was four, we dressed them in their very best clothes and took the train to the city and went to the Showgrounds from there. Large crowds of parents with children were waiting at the tram stop. Goldie and Jack were excited to be with such a large group of happy children; it was the first time they had been to the show. The weather was beautiful, and the farmers had brought all kinds of farm animals to the show – sheep, pigs, cows and more. They milked their cows and distributed free milk to the children at the Showground. We bought show bags filled with a lot of goodies. There were several sideshows and a lot of advertising. It was noisy and crowded but we had a very good time and for many years we never missed going to the Melbourne Show.

Every year on Boxing Day we went to the city with the children. We looked at the beautiful Christmas windows in Myers on Bourke Street. There was the Tivoli Theater nearby, also on Bourke Street, where they played live pantomimes for children. There was always a big queue for tickets, but it was worth the wait. The pantomimes were very entertaining and there was a different show every year, like "Cinderella" or "Snow White and the Seven Dwarfs." The theater was beautifully decorated, the children's costumes so colorful; the dancing and singing were excellent. We felt as if we were in a dream world.

In 1952, we celebrated with a very large crowd in Melbourne city when Queen Elizabeth was crowned. In 1956, when the Olympic Games came to Melbourne, we took the tram to the Olympic Village where we met the athletes and had a lot of fun. We saw the Queen's Mother in an open car waving to the public and we all loved her wonderful smile.

Whenever we had free time, we went into the city, to Coles' Restaurant on Bourke Street. There, we saw many people, all of them well dressed, enjoying the best of food. We realized that we were very lucky to be there as well. We thanked God that we lived in such a good country and that here, in Australia, we could finally be treated as equals to the people around us.

We had picnics in the Fitzroy Gardens and took the number 15 tram down to St. Kilda beach every Sunday (we still did not own a car). We also often visited the Botanical Gardens in Melbourne. I still visit these gardens and consider them to be the most beautiful in the world. I love everything in them, the whole panorama, the colorful varieties of flowers, and most of all I love the large, majestic trees, especially the Australian native trees.

To this day, when I walk through the splendor of the gardens, I cannot help but think that people with all their intelligence could never create such beauty – only nature. Those tall, strong, magnificent trees outlive many generations of people. Trees fulfil all that is required of them. They give us beauty, aroma, shade from the sun, cover from the wind, fresh air to breathe and a place for the birds' nests. It is in the tranquility of gardens that people's souls are soothed. They can forget their problems, and regardless of their age, they can feel happy and carefree, enjoying the moment and the simplicity of nature and all it offers to the world.

THE HARDSHIPS OF STARTING A TINY FACTORY
APOLLO KNITTING MILLS

Only one tram stop away from our house on Mitchell Street in Brunswick, on the corner of Holmes Street and Moreland Road, was a dry-cleaning shop. Behind the shop, a friend of my husband Chaim worked on knitting machines. Chaim and this man used to work together in a big knitting factory on Rathdowne Street. The man told Chaim that he was going to vacate the premises because he had bought newer fashion machines that needed a bigger space.

My husband liked the idea of renting this factory, but his friend could not rent out the premises to us, because he was only a sub-tenant. He told us to try Palters Dry Cleaners as the manager rented the whole building, but he only used the front for the dry-cleaning shop. When this friend vacated the factory, because we could not speak fluent English, we took our cousin Toiba with us to talk to the manager. He agreed to rent out the back of the shop to us, and we opened the factory, Apollo Knitting Mills, a few months later. I am not sure where the name came from, perhaps it was suggested by the registry when my husband registered the business, making us an official business entity.

We only had money for one knitting machine, and we needed six. What we also needed was a partner. A wealthy man offered to lend us money, but he wanted to be a silent partner. We rejected his proposal – we needed another couple like us who would work and share everything equally.

Auntie Rachel had a son, Max, whom she loved very much. He was single and he lived with his mother. He had never done a day's work, yet he dressed like a gentleman in a nice suit and fedora hat. Each morning Max went with his pals from the army to a club in the city to play cards with money his mother earned working. She never complained, in fact the opposite, she used to praise him as a genius. Yet, he was a likeable fellow. He was familiar with machines because he loved to pull Rachel's old sewing machine to pieces and then put it together again, but we were reluctant to have him as a partner.

We asked his sister Toiba and her husband Moshe if they would like to start working with us in the factory. We were experienced, we would teach them, and they would lend us the money. Toiba agreed straight away, because she dreamed of working in her own factory after working for others for many years. But Moshe didn't.

Auntie Rachel saw an opportunity for Max to work for the first time. She offered to lend us money on the condition that Max and Toiba would be equal partners with me and my husband. We agreed and went to a solicitor to make a special agreement that included paying back the loan from Auntie Rachel.

We bought five more 12-gauge flat knitting machines and a buttonhole machine, although to get the machines immediately we had to pay extra. So, we had the factory, the machines. But what about work? Toiba and I looked in the telephone book for addresses of warehouses, and we walked the streets for days but nobody gave us any work.

I had quit a good job, so had my husband, and we had a lot of debts to pay off for the machines, and for our house on Mitchell Street. The house was very old and dirty and in need of repair but there was no income. We hired a painter, but as he started to paint the heavy dry plaster from the ceilings and walls began to fall off. The only thing I could do was pray to God for help, and it came as a lucky break.

The last on our list of warehouses was Reinish and Enker, who owned a business called Renko. They were two elderly gentlemen who were refugees from Austria. I talked and they listened, especially Mr. Enker. He was not educated, but he was a good businessman, and he had a good heart. He said, "I will try your work." He gave us a big box of wool and a sample of a button-up ladies' cardigan. We were so very grateful and happy. We advertised for workers, and many came, and we started our factory at last. Reinish and Enker used to buy a lot of wool and supplied boxes of it to about six knitting factories. They hired a carrier with a van who delivered the wool to the factories and collected our ready cardigans every Friday. At the end of the year a businessman from interstate used to come and give them a cheque.

Next door to Mr. Enker lived a nice lady whose sister and her husband had recently arrived from England. The husband could not find a job. She described him as very presentable, tall, educated, an accountant, and said he could drive a van. Coincidentally, the usual carrier came to tell us that after he had collected a full van of finished knitwear, he had gone to buy a drink from a milk bar and when he came out his van had been stolen.

During the busy season, we worked 20 hours a day and slept for only four hours. It was not easy for my children, not having grandparents available to help, and having parents who worked all the time. In school, my daughter Goldie and my son Jack were top of the class. A friend, whose son attended Moreland State School with my son, used to scold me whenever she saw me for not attending a special day at school when the teacher had praised Jack for finishing top in class. My children always knew the real situation. They knew that it was my responsibility to keep the factory going and that if we did not deliver the supply of cardigans the new boss required every week, he would take the work away from us and give the wool to other factories. So they never complained.

I was trying to do my best under the circumstances. There was always plenty of food in the house; I cooked soups with potatoes, oats and lamb shanks, or cabbage soup, potatoes and cauliflower. On the weekends I did the laundry in cement troughs and boiled it in a gas copper for an hour or more.

One day, as I was taking out the laundry from the gas copper with a heavy wooden stick and putting it in the cement troughs, Jack, who was four years old, ran under me. I did not see him, and a few boiling water drops fell on his head. I took him by tram to a doctor who gave us some ointment, but it did not help. When I saw pus on the pillow, I knew the burn had become infected, so I took Jack to the Royal Children's Hospital. They called a doctor who gave him a special ointment, and it soon healed. I have since then contributed to every Good Friday Appeal for the Royal Children's Hospital.

OUR CORNER SHOP

In the late 1960s, our partner Toiba wished to retire. She asked us to pay out her share from the factory, but we refused and told her that she could take the machinery, wool and cotton, but we would not pay her. So in the middle of the busy season Toiba did not come to work. Instead, she went on a holiday.

Toiba was the only cutter, and the workers were waiting. I was not proficient in cutting but turned on the electric cutting machine and began cutting. Suddenly, I saw blood running from my finger. I put some cotton wool around it and took a tram to the Royal Melbourne Hospital. A junior doctor gave me a tetanus injection. Sweat was running from his forehead, but he sewed about 20 small stitches on my finger. He assured me that it would heal well.

My husband and I discussed the situation with Toiba. We were grateful to Auntie Rachel and her children for helping us when we arrived in Australia, for giving us the big pram to carry the children over the streets of Melbourne, for providing dinners when we lived three months in Cousin Sara's house. We were grateful to her two daughters, Libby and Toiba, for going with me to translate whenever I needed it. So, we decided we would pay Toiba her share as she asked.

Toiba's brother Max started estimating Toiba's share of the machines, the wool, the cotton, the buttons and it came to 2,500.00 pounds. Toiba took the cheque and bought a double-story boarding house on Drummond Street in Carlton. She received rent and was happy. Not long after Toiba's retirement, Renko went into liquidation. We had no liquid assets. We had also paid off our cousin Max for his share in the factory. All that was left were the machines, but these were old and obsolete, and we were left without an income. No one wanted to buy the machines, so a mechanic took them off our hands for nothing to use them as spare parts.

We had no money to pay for the factory, the house, food, or the children's education. I prayed to God for help.

My husband insisted I ask the manager of Palters Dry Cleaners, to whom we paid rent for the factory, if he would consider leasing the dry-cleaning shop that was in front of our factory to us. I did not want to ask the manager as my English was not good enough, but my husband drove me to the manager's office and insisted that I go in and ask. The manager said he would let us know. Before long he came to see us and told us that he had been making a loss, the shop was vacant, and he would rent it to us.

I believed it was a miracle, because at the same time we received a letter from Chaim's brother Mordechai, from Montevideo, Uruguay (who left Poland before the war) telling us that he had sent 4,000 dollars to an Australian bank for Chaim to collect. Chaim's other brother Avramel also lived in Melbourne and Chaim loved him very much, but they grew apart over the years, although they had survived the war together, hidden by a Polish farmer, Kalinowski, in Bruszewo.

Chaim took me to the carpenter's factory in Richmond where Avramel worked and told him that their brother Mordechai had sent him 4,000 dollars, but that he would not collect it till Avramel went with him and accepted half the money.

Now we had 2,000 dollars to start the shop. We went to the Zora Fashions factory on High Street, St. Kilda, owned by European Jews who were honest and kind people. I picked out a few dozen blouses; I had an eye for fashion and experience and knowledge about the quality of material from the ORT school in Bialystok, Poland, where I had studied dressmaking. The blouses we purchased from Zora were all different colors and styles. I hung them in the windows of the shop; they looked beautiful.

There were lots of factories where mainly women worked near our shop. They often came to look at our colorful display after work or during their lunch breaks. Although they did not have great incomes, they would put the blouses on lay-buy, and collect them when they got paid on Fridays. Every week I displayed different garments in the window and made them look enticing and attractive. The shop became very popular with the women from all the factories.

Many people came to the shop. We opened each morning at seven o'clock so people could drop in their dry cleaning on the way to work. Sometimes people came in to warm themselves while they waited for their factories to open. On Moreland Road there were many other shops: a news agency, cake shops and other essential stores. The shop workers also came to our shop to buy clothes.

The shop itself was not large. There was a big wooden counter with an old-fashioned cash register with lots of buttons on it. We did not know how to use it and just used a simple drawer below the counter instead. There were open shelves at the front of the shop that displayed jumpers that were knitted at the back of the shop by my husband. My husband also knitted children's sweaters and I sewed them up on the overlock machine. People who had large families of many children blessed us for selling the sweaters at such a good price.

During the 1960s, Australia converted to a decimal currency with dollars and cents; one pound to two dollars, one shilling to ten cents, one penny to one cent. It took people a long time to get used to the change. In the beginning, when I changed the price of a dress from ten pounds to 20 dollars, it seemed so expensive that people were reluctant to buy but they soon adapted to the change.

In the 1960s I also noticed that attitudes and fashions were changing. It was a time of economic prosperity in Australia, but it was also a time of social revolution where traditional values were being questioned. Clothes, hairstyles, and music changed a lot from the 1950s. Many of my customers were teenagers and young women. I decided to adopt the new fashions in my store and stocked very short skirts and dresses. My husband was a bit concerned about whether they would be successful, but it turned out to be a good decision. Young women loved the mini skirts and dresses, as did older women. After a short while, I was only selling miniskirts and dresses!

Our stock was shelved behind handmade curtains to keep the shop tidy. The linoleum on the floor was peeling and it could have done with a modern renovation, but the atmosphere inside was always pleasant and happy. You could hear many languages and broken English spoken in lots of different accents in the shop. Most of our customers were female immigrants from war-torn countries: Germans, Poles, Ukrainians, Yugoslavians, Italians, Greeks, Turks, Arabs and many, many more. They had endured difficult times before migrating to Australia and some had also suffered from persecution, just like we had in the Holocaust. In Australia, they found new lives, just like us. Australia was an example of shared humanity. Australia was the best example that different nationalities can live and work together in peace, friendship and respect. The prophecy from the Bible about the wolf lying down with the lamb and living in peace was fulfilled in Australia before my own eyes.

There was love and friendship in my shop; I felt a deep connection with most of my customers. They would tell me about their problems, and I would try to help them the best I could. I would say a little prayer for them; I would repair their clothing without charge. I helped poor women with many children. One customer came to the shops with six of her ten children and was crying. She told me that her husband was sick and could not work so she had sent two of her older girls – one 12 and one 13 years old – to work instead of school, and now she had received a letter telling her she had to go to court. She was very frightened. She had to take the six younger children to court with her, but she had no money and was ashamed of how they were dressed. I took six knitted jumpers from my shelf, and we put them on the children. I gave them to her as a present. The children looked very nice, and the woman felt a bit happier about going to court.

I gave credit to a lot of people. At the end of each year, at Christmas time, I crossed off all the debts that were outstanding. I started each new year with a clean slate. I took pride in doing so and felt glad that I could contribute to my customer-friends' happiness. I tried always to be truthful and honest in all my dealings with my customers in the shop and all the people I encountered throughout my life.

MOZART STREET, ST KILDA

Our house on Mitchell Street in Brunswick was in a very good location, but it was very old and in need of major repairs. We tried to do some important repairs and hired a carpenter to help my husband Chaim build a bigger kitchen over the weekends. They opened a few walls and discovered the long timber supporting the ceiling was too short and the ceiling sagged badly in the middle. We looked at the ceiling and decided to sell the house.

In about 1958, we bought a vacant house at 12 Mozart Street, St Kilda at auction. By that time, many members of the Jewish community had left the northside suburbs of Melbourne and moved to the southside, to the St Kilda, Elwood and Caulfield areas where there were bigger blocks and an established Jewish community. The children attended Elwood High School where many of the students were Jewish.

We soon purchased a Holden car and together with our friends we visited rural areas for picnics on weekends and holidays. We often went to Geelong beach in the summertime. Geelong was a small village then, with very few streets, but the beach was clean and beautiful. We also visited Sorrento and the Dandenongs.

In the late 60s, we spent the Christmas holidays in a motel near Healesville. This motel was built in the middle of a paddock. It had a milk-bar, a restaurant, a hall and small rooms. The Australian holiday guests organized a Christmas party and invited us to join them, and we had a nice time. We spent one holiday at a hotel called the Gypsy Princess, in Sherbrooke Forest. Our friends, also survivors, joined us. At dinnertime there was live music, and people danced. We enjoyed life whenever we could.

We had a lovely neighbor, Mr. F who had a wife and two children the same age as our daughter and son. Mr. F had survived several concentration camps and now he worked as a tailor and had a shop on Sydney Road in Brunswick where he sold men's suits and swimwear. He also did a lot of repairs and alterations. He knew his way around Victoria and took us to many places. He took us to Frankston, which in the 1960s was empty with no shops, only sand. There was only one bakery, so we bought fresh rolls and went to the beach. He also took us to Phillip Island for a holiday. One evening we went to see the penguins; they came out of the water waddling on two legs like little people, very orderly, and it was a pleasure to watch them.

I felt that Mr. F needed to be treated delicately and with respect after all that he had endured. He worked very long hours, but his wife did not work at all, which was unusual for an immigrant family, even then. Mr. F often arrived home from work to find that there was no dinner for him. He would sometimes come over to our house in the evenings and we could see that he was upset and hungry, so he ate with us. Perhaps his wife was unwell, and he could not provide her with support. Perhaps he was unwell, and she could not handle him. In those days, no one really had counseling for the trauma that they had suffered as a result of the Holocaust.

Mr. F's wife left for a holiday to visit her sister and he could not cope with her absence; he must have been haunted by the demons of his past. It was not smooth sailing by any means for a lot of Holocaust survivors. The past was always inside us. Shortly after Mr. F's wife returned from overseas, he killed himself. He jumped from St. Kilda Beach bridge into the sea. We were devastated.

MY CHILDREN GROW UP

When my husband and I came home from work we would have dinner with the children at the table, but suddenly our son Jack stopped eating at home. I noticed that he and his friend Adi chose to go to a Chinese restaurant on Acland Street, where they ate dim sims and other food we had never heard of before. My husband was very upset and wondered how Jack would be able to survive without traditional food. He insisted I take the boy to Dr. Lewick on Mitchell Street, close to the factory. Reluctantly, I took Jack to the doctor who heard my story and agreed that he should be left alone, that he would be perfectly alright.

Jack was a black belt in Judo. He was also the Victorian weightlifting champion in the junior division. Nearly all of his classmates had cars called "old bombs." Every few nights they used to wake up Jack to help them push an old bomb that had broken down in the middle of a road somewhere.

One such episode I witnessed myself. Our car was being repaired and the owner of the repair shop loaned us an old car to travel to work. It was a Saturday evening and the whole family was going to a friend's party in Kew in this old car. On the Punt Road hill, the car stopped. We jumped out as the car started to run downhill. Cars were coming towards us; I panicked and grabbed at the car to stop it – it was hopping like a fly. Then I saw a real miracle. My son Jack ran after the car and jumped in and turned off the ignition. He stopped it with his bare hands. He had strength like Samson from the Bible.

Often Jack came home very late, but he continued with his studies, and he won a scholarship to Melbourne University to do medicine. My daughter Goldie also excelled in school. She was accepted to study law at the University of Melbourne at a time when there were very few women who studied law, let alone, went to university. We encouraged her to study, and we were so proud of her.

A highlight of our life was the engagement of my daughter Goldie to Victor Kelmann, a medical student; it was a most wonderful and enjoyable occasion. This was in 1965, and we celebrated with a supper dance in the New Empire Ballroom on Chapel Street, Prahran. The orchestra was called Vollaro and the singer, Tony Corenzo, sang such beautiful romantic songs that made the girls swoon. The food supplied by the owners, Weinberg and Erwbergy, was of the best quality, as were the drinks we supplied. My daughter looked gorgeous. Victor looked handsome and they were both very happy.

The dancing never stopped, and the singing was terrific. People waited in a line to get cards from the musicians so they could book them for their own special occasions. We had lost so many family members and friends, and now we were enlarging our family through marriage. It was a dream come true. We ordered the same hall for the wedding that was booked for December 11, 1966.

While Goldie and Victor were on their honeymoon, my husband and I looked for a flat to rent for them. We found a nice one in St. Kilda. We bought furniture, a mattress and base, and we ordered a special eiderdown with satin covers, cushions, dishes, spoons and all other necessities. We paid rent and bond money, and they moved in. When they came back from their honeymoon my daughter told me that she was pregnant. After the baby girl, Marilyn, was born we bought a pram, and each weekend Goldie and Victor brought the baby to our house so we could look after her while the young couple could go out and enjoy themselves. She was given the Yiddish name Malka after Goldie's husband's late mother who was killed in the Holocaust. I felt so proud when I walked with the baby, and I wondered if our friends were jealous and wished that their daughters had a baby so they could be happy grandparents like us.

My son started to go out with girls too. One was too tall, one was too small, but he eventually met the right one. Hanna Feldpicer was both pretty and nice. They got engaged and later married. As the family grew, I tried to help by inviting them to dinners on Friday nights and looking after the babies on the weekends.

My daughter Goldie was interested in buying two units in Elwood that were to be auctioned with a compulsory $8,000 deposit, regardless of the auction sale price. My husband gave me $500 and sent me by tram to the auction. My son-in-law Victor brought a bank book containing $300. We were the highest bidders, and we bought the two houses for a total of $36,000. The auctioneer demanded a deposit of $8,000, but my daughter being a lawyer explained that we believed that the deposit was 10 percent of that, making it $800. She paid my son-in law $300 and my $500 which amounted to exactly $800, the auctioneer agreed, and they signed the contract. They later renovated one house for medical practice and the second house to live in. Soon, they had two more children – Fiona and Anthony. Fiona was given the Yiddish name Feigele, named after my husband's late mother.

Hanna soon gave birth to a girl Sharon and then a couple of years later became pregnant with twins. Two boys were born, not identical, one blond named Brian, the other one darker, called Phillip. A year later Goldie also had a baby boy, Anthony. My husband and I were very happy and felt blessed to have six beautiful grandchildren. We had many birthday parties. I used to buy remnants and make dresses or pajamas for the babies; I always looked in the shops for children's clothing. I loved my family so much, and I was grateful for everything. I knew that the children were a present from God, and my way of pleasing God and showing my gratitude for his gifts is to be show kindness to all people, regardless of what they have or do not have, and regardless of their race or religion.

When our children were already grown up, our friends started to arrange holidays through travel agencies to Surfers Paradise in Queensland. Chaim and I and another couple arranged a holiday in the Chevron Hotel, which was the most popular hotel in the 1970s. It was the middle of July, and while Melbourne was cold, Surfer's Paradise had beautiful sunny weather. The rooms in the hotel were not very modern, but nobody stayed inside for long, so it really did not matter.

Breakfast was from eight to ten o'clock in the big dining room where the best food was served. There was orange juice, bacon and eggs, bread, butter, jam, coffee, fish, and porridge. Most people knew each other, so lively conversations started between them.

After breakfast, most people went to the swimming pool where some went swimming, and some rested in the lounges. My husband and I used to go by bus to Pacific Fair, a newly built, modern shopping center. Free buses ran to new casinos where we used to go and have a lot of fun with free entertainment, pokies and lunch. On Fridays we took a bus to Southport, which was a nice clean town with very nice shops, interesting cafés and good food.

The years flew past, and the grandchildren were growing up. When my oldest granddaughter was about 18, I talked to my daughter about marriage. She laughed at me and said that marriage was not fashionable anymore. I remembered long ago, when I was a young girl, how my mother and all the other mothers in my town felt their biggest problem was how to save money for their daughter's dowries. There were already "old maids" in some families, women who had once been young and pretty, but that nobody would marry without a dowry. I talked to my husband about this, and we felt that even here in Australia money would help children to think about marriage.

As soon as we had some money saved, we gave half to my son and half to my daughter on the condition that they use it for a deposit on a property for their older daughters. And it happened that soon after my eldest granddaughter married, and my son's daughter also married. When we were sitting at the main table in the best reception halls at our grandchildren's weddings, it was the greatest happiness and pleasure for me and my husband.

Every Sunday my husband and I took the car, picked up a friend who had recently lost her husband and went to the Botanical Gardens. A lot of people of all nationalities were there, and there were families with children, older people with grandchildren, and very old people whose families were taking them on outings from nursing homes or from their lonely units. We used to meet friends and chat, go for walks or just sit on a bench and watch other people.

Intermarriage was frightening for people of all nationalities. In my shop I often heard mothers crying that their son or daughter was marrying someone of a different nationality, and they found it very distressing. One Sunday afternoon in the '70s, I witnessed a tragedy caused by intermarriage whilst out at my weekly visit to the Botanical Gardens. A close friend of ours had two sons. One son had married a woman of the same nationality, and they had two children. The other son was never mentioned. We were sitting at the entrance to the gardens and talking with our friends. Suddenly the woman stood up and ran to a couple who had come into the gardens with a baby in their arms. She kissed them and cried, and I believed that they were some friends she had not seen for a long time.

My friend's husband stood up briskly and walked away. When our friend returned, she told us that the couple were her son and his wife and their week-old baby daughter. The son's wife was from a different nationality and his father could not forgive him for it, but she, with a mother's heart, could not hide her love any longer and made peace with her son and his family. From that day on she kept inviting them to her home and her husband at last made peace with his son and his family.

The son's family grew bigger, and our friend was close to his beautiful family. When the older girl was about eight years old, our friend, her grandmother, took her for a walk in a park close to her house. As they walked, she saw a neighbor sitting on a bench, who didn't know that her son had a wife of a different nationality and that they had children so she tried to avoid the woman; the little girl understood what was going on, and she asked, "Nana, are you avoiding this woman because of me, are you ashamed of me?" That's when our friend took the child by the hand and went to this woman and said, "This is my beautiful granddaughter!" The child was happy, and I liked and respected our friend even more.

In 1985, my husband Chaim and I packed two very heavy suitcases and took the bus from Elizabeth Street to Melbourne Airport. We had booked a flat for three weeks in Centrepoint, Surfers Paradise. We arrived at Coolangatta Airport and waited to collect our suitcases. The carousel was rolling around and we missed one turn, so next time when my husband saw our suitcases coming past, he grabbed them with such force that he busted a muscle. He had weak muscles and had had two hernia operations, but he forgot to be careful. He was covered in sweat and in terrible pain, but he was convinced the pain would stop.

The pain did not stop. We waited for two days, and then I cancelled the scheduled return flight time and rebooked our tickets to return to Melbourne sooner. As soon as we arrived, we went to see Dr. Cherny, and he called an ambulance to take Chaim to the Alfred Hospital. The doctors diagnosed a coronary heart attack. They gave him a lot of tablets and sent him home. Later he had a series of hospital and medical treatments, and I was so absorbed with my dear husband that I did not think about myself.

On July 31, 2000, my dear husband Chaim died after continued bad health and something inside of me died with him. I felt all churned up, nothing interested me, nothing was important. I was restless and could not stay at home alone. Every morning, I ran to old people's clubs, but I could not calm down. My beautiful children and wonderful grandchildren tried to help me. I kept praying to God asking him to help me, to let me calm down. The children sacrificed their weekends to take me out. My daughter took me with her wherever she was invited.

Every Saturday morning my daughter took me shopping, and then to her place for lunch. My son took me to Shabbat dinners at his children's homes or to restaurants every Friday night. My son also suffered greatly from the recent tragic loss of his wife Hanna. She died of breast cancer at the age of 48. Despite this pain, he and his children helped me cope. All my grandchildren gave up their time to take me out and visit me. They took me to the supermarket, out to lunch and visited me regularly.

It was very hard for my children to take me from Ormond where I lived to Toorak where they lived, and then to bring me back at night. They tried to tell me that it would be best to sell my house and to buy an apartment close to where they lived. At first, I was reluctant, but later I agreed. A real estate agent took over the sale of my house in Ormond, and my daughter took me every weekend to look for an apartment. We looked for a unit, but they were small, old and far from public transport. So, we started looking at apartments, some were too expensive, some not nice, until we found a nice apartment next to a tram stop. It was a high-rise building with a lift and the body-corporate was going to renovate the whole building of 34 flats.

When I first moved to my new apartment, I was in pain from hip arthritis so I could not walk properly, and I was lonely. I didn't know any of the neighbors, and because the building was being renovated there was noise and dust everywhere. The old air conditioners were removed and were to be replaced but inside the flat the heat was unbearable. Most people who lived in the apartment block used to leave in the mornings and come back at night when the workers with the noisy machines left, but I had to stay inside the dusty noise and heat or cold because I couldn't walk. The renovation lasted for nine months.

The pain got worse. Twice a week the agent organized inspections of the house, so everything had to stay in order, and when the time came to move and I had to reach to the top shelves to do sorting and packing, it didn't help my arthritis. I took tablets, Vioxx and Panadol, and had injections for pain. I went to Cedar Court for physiotherapy and for hydrotherapy, but nothing helped. The pain was unbearable. I couldn't lift my legs. It looked like this was the end, but my belief in heavenly help never faded, and I talked and prayed with all my heart.

I remembered when I was in Poland when the Germans occupied the land and began to kill all the Jews, how I was saved with heavenly miracles and hoped that I could be saved again. Several people advised me to go to a medical specialist and have an operation on my hips. My children agreed that I should make an appointment for a hip operation. I had one operation, and it was excellent. The pain stopped in that leg and I could move it again. The pain in the other leg was still there so the specialist suggested he should operate on the other leg, and I agreed.

I was happy again. Now not only did I have new windows, new air conditioning, new painting, I also had new hips and soon I had new beautiful, good-hearted friends. These were women who lived in the building; they were also Holocaust survivors. We went out for coffee almost every day together to Funkie's Cafe and Laurent Bakery in the Toorak village and took turns cooking lunch for each other. I was not lonely anymore.

I believe that we all have a guardian angel in Heaven who is waiting to hear our cry for help, but to be heard we must be connected. In order for that to happen, we must be humble, generous, just, fair and keep the Ten Commandments. Whenever my family and friends are desperate for help, and think they will never be heard in Heaven, I assure them that we should believe in a greater power that is going to look after us. We should never lose hope.

REUNION IN ISRAEL 1971

In December 1971, Chaim and I closed our shop for eight weeks. We packed two big boxes and sent them to Israel as excess baggage. We took two suitcases and left for Israel by plane. I wanted to see with my own eyes the miracle that God had performed for the Jews. From the remnants, from lonely survivors scattered all over the world, from the hell of the gas chambers and from the holes in the forests, God had created a nation, just like He promised He would in the Bible.

I also wanted to see the people I was with during the war, the partisans and the Jews who hid in the forests and bunkers. A lot of them had settled in Israel and established a new, free generation that was ready to fight and give their lives for their own country, for Israel.

We arrived at Lod Airport. It was a sunny day, and I was so excited that I wanted to drop down and kiss the ground. I looked around me and saw Jewish soldiers, Jewish police and Jewish officials, all of them speaking Hebrew, the holy language of the Bible, of the prophets, of King David.

A large group of people was waiting for us at the airport. I saw my Uncle Abraham-Moshe, my father's brother, who lives in Israel with his wife whom he met and married in Bialystok, his two beautiful daughters, and two granddaughters. The younger daughter was a fashion writer for a magazine, and she traveled regularly to Paris. She married a fellow fashion writer. A tragedy befell the older daughter Ahuva's husband. He was killed on the football field when he suffered a bad head injury. She remarried a good man who helped her raise her two daughters.

I saw Moshe Maik, who survived in the bunker with my husband, his wife Sarah, and Faigele Tabak, my little cousin, now grown up, with her husband Hilik. Faigele Tabak, the daughter of Manes and Lea, with whom I lived in the Sokoly ghetto during the war, emigrated to Israel after the war. She survived the war thanks to the good Polish woman Piekutowska. Her parents and all her siblings were murdered in the Holocaust, and she was the sole survivor. She served in the Israel defense forces and became known as *Tzippora*, the Hebrew equivalent of Faigele, meaning "little bird." She married a *Sabra* [a native-born Israeli], Hilik (Yechiel) Burstein. He is from a large family, all of them proud citizens of a free land. Hilik's brother is a general in the Israeli Army, and Hilik himself is a high-ranking officer, Lieutenant-Colonel, who has served tirelessly in the armed forces and intelligence units of the Israeli Defence Forces.

We went to stay with Faigele and her family in Ramat Gan, a suburb near Tel Aviv. They have three lovely children: Menachem (named after her father Manes), Leah (named after her mother) and Gili, a modern Hebrew girl's name. At the time of writing, they have ten grandchildren. Our families have remained in close contact throughout the years and when my family always stays at their home when they visit Israel; this is reciprocated in Australia.

We rested for a bit, then went to meet the survivors from the Bransk Forest. We traveled to Haifa to see Haim Velvel Pribut, who brought us food in the forest when he was a young boy. He had a wife and two daughters, but he was now a very sick man.

In Melbourne, before we departed for the trip to Israel, Luba Olenski, who remained my dear friend ever since we met as partisans together in the Bransk forest, gave me some money to give to Haim Velvel Pribut. We hoped that this, along with some money that I gave him, would improve his comfort for a while.

We went to Kiryat Bialystok, a small village suburb of Yehud, a town situated not far from Tel Aviv. Kiryat Bialystok is named after the city of Bialystok in Poland, whose 60,000 Jews were killed by the German Nazis between 1941 and 1945. Kiryat Bialystok is a village full of Jewish life. The older generation speaks Yiddish as well as Hebrew, but the younger generation speaks only Hebrew.

Matel Finkelstein lives in Kiryat Bialystok with her son, Avramele. Avramele married a *Sefardi* [Oriental Jewish] girl, and they have three daughters. He owns an abattoir where they prepare meat for the butcher shops. Matel's daughter, Shoshka, lives nearby with her husband, Velvel Halpern. They have two lovely daughters and one son. Shoshka owns a butcher shop in Yehud, not far from Kiryat Bialystok. Matel's younger daughter, the blonde Chanale, also lives in Yehud. She is married and has two daughters.

Matel told me that when she ran away from the Bransk ghetto in 1942, her baby – a beautiful, blonde little girl – was 18 months old. Matel took the baby to a Polish woman to hide her from the Germans. When Matel returned to collect her daughter after the war, the woman told her that she had been frightened to keep the baby and so she had taken her to the church orphanage in Bialystok.

In 1945, Matel went to Bialystok to look for her child, without success. Nobody knew anything about the little girl. Matel spent days and weeks just sitting and watching the children from the orphanage when they went out for walks, hoping and praying that she would recognize her daughter. Finally, she had to leave. She went to Israel without knowing what had happened to her daughter. After surviving the war, Matel's husband, Chaim Finkelstein, was killed by Polish bandits.

Moshe Kleinot and his wife Esther, from Ciechanowiec, also live in Kiryat Bialystok, not far from Shoshka. Esther survived the war by hiding in the forests. They have two daughters. Their son was killed in the Yom Kippur War, in 1973.

It was a Saturday afternoon, a lovely sunny day. People were walking up and down the streets talking to each other, looking at the lovely gardens and beautiful homes, sharing jokes with one another. There was laughter and happiness all around. It was a very happy and free atmosphere, just like it had been in my hometown, Ciechanowiec, before the war.

At Shoshka's house, they were preparing for a party to be held in our honor. Matel brought cholent. Many guests were invited. Srulke Brenner and his wife came from Haifa. Esterke, the redhead from the bunker, was also there with her husband, who works in the law courts. They have two beautiful daughters, one of whom was chosen to be Miss Israel. We were all very happy. We sat around, singing. We were very grateful that we all had survived and were able to meet again in our own, free homeland.

We went to Jerusalem to see Moshe Rubinstein, Gittel's son, a good and honest man. He is a policeman, and his wife also works at the police station. They have two daughters and live in a very nice flat. Moshe is happy to have the privilege of helping to protect the Holy City.

He told me news of other people from the Bransk Forest: Moshe's sister Kikla married Pelchowitz. They live on a farm and work on the land. Simcha Pam married a girl named Leah who survived Auschwitz. They also have a farm. Little Stella from the forest also lives in Jerusalem. She married a doctor, and they have a lovely family.

Yossel Broida was a courageous and happy young man in the forest. He was happy because he was not alone; his younger brother, Yitzhak (Itchale), a handsome, happy 17-year-old, was with him. He used to sing romantic songs and we all loved him. Both brothers survived the war, but soon after it ended, Itchale Broida was killed by the Polish AK. After that, Yossel was no longer the same man. He left Poland with a curse on his lips. He married an American woman and now lives with his family in Venezuela but often visits Israel.

My husband's cousin, Moshe Maik, with whom he survived in the bunker during the Holocaust, lives in Netanya. He is a very fine man. Moshe and his wife, Sarah, have a wonderful family: one daughter and three sons. Moshe owns a shop where he sells radios, televisions, and other electrical appliances. Everybody likes to buy from him because he is honest. He is also very generous and friendly, and his door is always open to visitors.

We went to visit the two daughters of my husband's uncle Tevie, who had emigrated to Israel before the war. The older daughter Adasa lived in Tel Aviv above a shop. She had a son and a daughter. The son was a truck driver, married with a baby daughter. The daughter did not want to serve in the Israeli Defense Forces, so she pretended to be very religious. She worked as a sales assistant in a shop. Her mother told us that she now regretted not sending her daughter to the army because it meant she did not have any friends her age and she was lonely. She was very beautiful. We understood that it would be traumatic to send a daughter to the army and we thought about the impact that the army had on people's lives. The other daughter Lea lived in Ashkelon, a city south of Tel Aviv. We traveled by taxi from the *Histradut* [trade union] because my uncle Abram-Moshe worked there but Lea was not home.

We visited Perec Buksztelsky, the son of Itka, my mother's best friend, a beautiful and generous lady who looked after me like her own daughter when I lived in Bialystok whilst studying at the ORT high school. I remembered this and as a small gesture we gave Itka's son Derec a Seiko watch and a few hundred dollars. He told me that he was in the Russian Army in 1941. At the beginning of the war, he was wounded, lying in a ditch somewhere, when a Russian Army tank truck stopped, picked him up and took him to a Russian hospital. After the war, he married a beautiful girl named Nina. Together, they came to Israel. They have one daughter and are very happy. The rest of his family were all murdered in the Holocaust.

EPILOGUE

My younger cousin, Toiba Tabak, with whom I survived as a partisan in the Bransk forest, survived the war. Afterwards, she went to Russia with Wanka Smyrno, from the partisan group. Wanka was in his thirties, and he had an existing wife and family. Toiba was pregnant with his child. When I was in Malaryta, I received a letter from Wanka, telling me that Toiba had died. To this day, I have never been able to find out exactly what happened to her. My heart aches for her. Perhaps her child, the only remnant of my Uncle Pesach and Aunt Sorcha, may be alive today somewhere.

The three Olenski brothers live in Melbourne. They deserve the highest respect and recognition; thanks to their help and care, over 70 Jews survived in the Bransk forest. David Olenski married Luba Frank, the Lithuanian girl from the forest. They have two sons and one daughter. Shlomo Olenski has a wife and two children, and Avraham Olenski remained single. The Olenskis's cousin, Dina Bender, also lives in Melbourne. She has a daughter and several grandsons.

Yankel (Jakob) Rubin, from the Bransk Forest, now lives in

Melbourne too. He married a survivor from a concentration camp. They have two children and several grandchildren.

Moshe Janczeman from the Bransk Forest died in Melbourne. He left a wife, daughter and grandchildren.

Moshe Oskard also died in Melbourne.

I compare my life to that of Job, as related in the Bible. Job lost everything he had, but after all his bad experiences he did not lose his belief in God, and he was rewarded. After all my terrible experiences, I, too, continue to believe in God with all my heart, and I, too, have been rewarded.

After I retired from work, I went to study English at the Melbourne Council of Adult Education. I wanted to write my story, but I needed to learn English first. I passed the year 12 English exams. In our year 12 class, we discussed my communication project about individuality. We all agreed that it is wrong to judge people by their nationalities or religions. In every nation, there are good and bad people. Everyone is an individual, and therefore one person cannot answer for anyone else who shares his or her nationality. In this God-given country, Australia, many different nationalities live together. We should all respect each other and preserve a friendly atmosphere. I decided to write this book so that my story could be told, and future generations could understand the dangers of hatred and prejudice.

I lost my whole family in the Holocaust. Now, God has blessed me with an honest, gentle husband, two children, and six beautiful grandchildren. My daughter, Goldie, completed law school. She is a talented and hard-working woman who helps many underprivileged people with their legal problems. She is married to a doctor, and they have three lovely children. My son, Jack, a good and very honest man, is a doctor and very active in Jewish communal sports. He married Hanna, a generous, kind-hearted and beautiful woman who is involved in several charities, and they have three lovely children.

I thank You, God, for allowing me to express my troubles and my pain in words. I thank You for the sunshine, for every breath, for my life. I am eternally grateful for the complete happiness I have achieved in my life.

MY MESSAGE

We all have a mission to fulfil in life. Our mission is to be friendly, to love, to be peaceful, to enjoy life, and to be grateful for the beauty of life. Our mission is to stop people from hating and killing others.

We should not be greedy, nor jealous, nor love money too much, because no amount of money can satisfy people and make them happy. We need true love and honest friendship, without regard for any reward or gain. Most of all, everyone should value the gift of life.

I believe that the main principle of religion is "Do unto others what you would have them do unto you." I know that there are many good people everywhere and that we can all live together in peace.

PHOTOS

Feigele Tabak, 1937

Toiba Tabak, prewar

Luba's grandmother Hinka Tabak, prewar

Chaim's youngest sister Toiba, 1940

Chaim, 1945

Luba with Feigele Tabak, Poland, 1945

Moshe Maik, 1946

Mr and Mrs Kalinoswki, the farmers who owned the property where the Goldberg brothers hid. Chaim Luba and Chaim kept in contact with them until their death and sent them regular parcels and money. Postwar.

Luba with baby Goldie and niece Feigele, circa 1946

Luba, Chaim and Goldie, 1947

Luba, with children Goldie and Jack, circa 1949

Feigele (Tzippora) in Israel, circa 1965

Luba, 1966

Goldie and Victor's wedding, 1966

Jack and Hanna's wedding, 1969

Chaim and Luba with Marilyn, 1970

Luba and Chaim in Queensland, circa 1978

Luba and Chaim, circa 1980

The three brothers. Left: Chaim Goldberg, middle: Mordechai Goldberg, right: Avremele Goldberg, 1982

Luba with children Goldie and Jack, circa 2002

Luba at the book launch for her memoir, 2004

Great-grandchildren, 2004

Luba with Luba Olenski, Melbourne, circa 2010

Luba surrounded by great-grandchildren, circa 2010

Luba and great-granddaughter Lucy, 2013

Luba surrounded by some of her great-grandchildren and granddaughters, 2013

Luba with some of her great-grand children, circa 2018

Luba, Fiona and Lucy at the Melbourne Holocaust Museum, 2016

Luba with granddaughters Marilyn, Fiona and Sharon, circa 2019

Luba surrounded by some of her great grand children, circa 2019

Luba with her children Jack and Goldie, 2022

AMSTERDAM PUBLISHERS
HOLOCAUST LIBRARY

The series **Holocaust Survivor Memoirs World War II** consists of the following autobiographies of survivors:

Outcry. Holocaust Memoirs, by Manny Steinberg

Hank Brodt Holocaust Memoirs. A Candle and a Promise, by Deborah Donnelly

The Dead Years. Holocaust Memoirs, by Joseph Schupack

Rescued from the Ashes. The Diary of Leokadia Schmidt, Survivor of the Warsaw Ghetto, by Leokadia Schmidt

My Lvov. Holocaust Memoir of a twelve-year-old Girl, by Janina Hescheles

Remembering Ravensbrück. From Holocaust to Healing, by Natalie Hess

Wolf. A Story of Hate, by Zeev Scheinwald with Ella Scheinwald

Save my Children. An Astonishing Tale of Survival and its Unlikely Hero, by Leon Kleiner with Edwin Stepp

Holocaust Memoirs of a Bergen-Belsen Survivor & Classmate of Anne Frank, by Nanette Blitz Konig

Defiant German - Defiant Jew. A Holocaust Memoir from inside the Third Reich, by Walter Leopold with Les Leopold

In a Land of Forest and Darkness. The Holocaust Story of two Jewish Partisans, by Sara Lustigman Omelinski

Holocaust Memories. Annihilation and Survival in Slovakia, by Paul Davidovits

From Auschwitz with Love. The Inspiring Memoir of Two Sisters' Survival, Devotion and Triumph Told by Manci Grunberger Beran & Ruth Grunberger Mermelstein, by Daniel Seymour

Remetz. Resistance Fighter and Survivor of the Warsaw Ghetto, by Jan Yohay Remetz

My March Through Hell. A Young Girl's Terrifying Journey to Survival, by Halina Kleiner with Edwin Stepp

Roman's Journey, by Roman Halter

Beyond Borders. Escaping the Holocaust and Fighting the Nazis. 1938-1948, by Rudi Haymann

The Engineers. A memoir of survival through World War II in Poland and Hungary, by Henry Reiss

Spark of Hope. An Autobiography, by Luba Wrobel Goldberg

Footnote to History. From Hungary to America. The Memoir of a Holocaust Survivor, by Andrew Laszlo

The series **Holocaust Survivor True Stories**
consists of the following biographies:

Among the Reeds. The true story of how a family survived the Holocaust, by Tammy Bottner

A Holocaust Memoir of Love & Resilience. Mama's Survival from Lithuania to America, by Ettie Zilber

Living among the Dead. My Grandmother's Holocaust Survival Story of Love and Strength, by Adena Bernstein Astrowsky

Heart Songs. A Holocaust Memoir, by Barbara Gilford

Shoes of the Shoah. The Tomorrow of Yesterday, by Dorothy Pierce

Hidden in Berlin. A Holocaust Memoir, by Evelyn Joseph Grossman

Separated Together. The Incredible True WWII Story of Soulmates Stranded an Ocean Apart, by Kenneth P. Price, Ph.D.

The Man Across the River. The incredible story of one man's will to survive the Holocaust, by Zvi Wiesenfeld

If Anyone Calls, Tell Them I Died. A Memoir, by Emanuel (Manu) Rosen

The House on Thrömerstrasse. A Story of Rebirth and Renewal in the Wake of the Holocaust, by Ron Vincent

Dancing with my Father. His hidden past. Her quest for truth. How Nazi Vienna shaped a family's identity, by Jo Sorochinsky

The Story Keeper. Weaving the Threads of Time and Memory - A Memoir, by Fred Feldman

Krisia's Silence. The Girl who was not on Schindler's List, by Ronny Hein

Defying Death on the Danube. A Holocaust Survival Story, by Debbie J. Callahan with Henry Stern

A Doorway to Heroism. A decorated German-Jewish Soldier who became an American Hero, by Rabbi W. Jack Romberg

The Shoemaker's Son. The Life of a Holocaust Resister, by Laura Beth Bakst

The Redhead of Auschwitz. A True Story, by Nechama Birnbaum

Land of Many Bridges. My Father's Story, by Bela Ruth Samuel Tenenholtz

Creating Beauty from the Abyss. The Amazing Story of Sam Herciger, Auschwitz Survivor and Artist, by Lesley Ann Richardson

On Sunny Days We Sang. A Holocaust Story of Survival and Resilience, by Jeannette Grunhaus de Gelman

Painful Joy. A Holocaust Family Memoir, by Max J. Friedman

I Give You My Heart. A True Story of Courage and Survival, by Wendy Holden

In the Time of Madmen, by Mark A. Prelas

Monsters and Miracles. Horror, Heroes and the Holocaust, by Ira Wesley Kitmacher

Flower of Vlora. Growing up Jewish in Communist Albania, by Anna Kohen

Aftermath: Coming of Age on Three Continents. A Memoir, by Annette Libeskind Berkovits

Not a real Enemy. The True Story of a Hungarian Jewish Man's Fight for Freedom, by Robert Wolf

Zaidy's War. Four Armies, Three Continents, Two Brothers. One Man's Impossible Story of Endurance, by Martin Bodek

The Glassmaker's Son. Looking for the World my Father left behind in Nazi Germany, by Peter Kupfer

The Apprentice of Buchenwald. The True Story of the Teenage Boy Who Sabotaged Hitler's War Machine, by Oren Schneider

Good for a Single Journey, by Helen Joyce

Burying the Ghosts. She escaped Nazi Germany only to have her life torn apart by the woman she saved from the camps: her mother, by Sonia Case

American Wolf. From Nazi Refugee to American Spy. A True Story, by Audrey Birnbaum

Bipolar Refugee. A Saga of Survival and Resilience, by Peter Wiesner

In the Wake of Madness. My Family's Escape from the Nazis, by Bettie Lennett Denny

Before the Beginning and After the End, by Hymie Anisman

I Will Give Them an Everlasting Name. Jacksonville's Stories of the Holocaust, by Samuel Cox

Hiding in Holland. A Resistance Memoir, by Shulamit Reinharz

The Ghosts on the Wall. A Grandson's Memoir of the Holocaust, by Kenneth D. Wald

The series **Jewish Children in the Holocaust** consists of the following
autobiographies of Jewish children
hidden during WWII in the Netherlands:

Searching for Home. The Impact of WWII on a Hidden Child,
by Joseph Gosler

Sounds from Silence. Reflections of a Child Holocaust Survivor,
Psychiatrist and Teacher, by Robert Krell

Sabine's Odyssey. A Hidden Child and her Dutch Rescuers,
by Agnes Schipper

The Journey of a Hidden Child, by Harry Pila and Robin Black

The series **New Jewish Fiction** consists of the following novels, written by Jewish authors. All novels are set in the time during or after the Holocaust.

The Corset Maker. A Novel, by Annette Libeskind Berkovits

Escaping the Whale. The Holocaust is over. But is it ever over for the next generation? by Ruth Rotkowitz

When the Music Stopped. Willy Rosen's Holocaust, by Casey Hayes

Hands of Gold. One Man's Quest to Find the Silver Lining in Misfortune, by Roni Robbins

The Girl Who Counted Numbers. A Novel, by Roslyn Bernstein

There was a garden in Nuremberg. A Novel, by Navina Michal Clemerson

The Butterfly and the Axe, by Omer Bartov

To Live Another Day. A Novel, by Elizabeth Rosenberg

A Worthy Life. Based on a True Story, by Dahlia Moore

The Right to Happiness. After all they went through. Stories, by Helen Schary Motro

The series **Holocaust Heritage** consists of the following memoirs by 2G:

The Cello Still Sings. A Generational Story of the Holocaust and of the Transformative Power of Music, by Janet Horvath

The Fire and the Bonfire. A Journey into Memory, by Ardyn Halter

The Silk Factory: Finding Threads of My Family's True Holocaust Story, by Michael Hickins

Winter Light. The Memoir of a Child of Holocaust Survivors, by Grace Feuerverger

Stumbling Stones, by Joanna Rosenthall

The Unspeakable. Breaking decades of family silence surrounding the Holocaust, by Nicola Hanefeld

Hidden in Plain Sight. A Journey into Memory and Place, by Julie Brill

The series **Holocaust Books for Young Adults** consists of the following novels, based on true stories:

The Boy behind the Door. How Salomon Kool Escaped the Nazis. Inspired by a True Story, by David Tabatsky

Running for Shelter. A True Story, by Suzette Sheft

The Precious Few. An Inspirational Saga of Courage based on True Stories, by David Twain with Art Twain

Dark Shadows Hover, by Jordan Steven Sher

The Sun will Shine on You again one Day, by Cynthia Monsour

The series **WWII Historical Fiction** consists of the following novels, some of which are based on true stories:

Mendelevski's Box. A Heartwarming and Heartbreaking Jewish Survivor's Story, by Roger Swindells

A Quiet Genocide. The Untold Holocaust of Disabled Children in WWII Germany, by Glenn Bryant

The Knife-Edge Path, by Patrick T. Leahy

Brave Face. The Inspiring WWII Memoir of a Dutch/German Child, by I. Caroline Crocker and Meta A. Evenbly

When We Had Wings. The Gripping Story of an Orphan in Janusz Korczak's Orphanage. A Historical Novel, by Tami Shem-Tov

Jacob's Courage. Romance and Survival amidst the Horrors of War, by Charles S. Weinblatt

A Semblance of Justice. Based on true Holocaust experiences, by Wolf Holles

This Grey Place, by Katie O'Connor

Amsterdam Publishers Newsletter

Subscribe to our Newsletter by selecting the menu at the top (right) of **amsterdampublishers.com** or scan the QR-code below.

Receive a variety of content such as:

- A welcome message by the founder
- Free Holocaust memoirs
- Book recommendations
- News about upcoming releases
- Chance to become an AP Reviewer.

www.ingramcontent.com/pod-product-compliance
Lightning Source LLC
LaVergne TN
LVHW041909070526
838199LV00051BA/2550